Best Easy Day Hikes
Long Island

Help Us Keep This Guide Up to Date

Every effort has been made by the author and editors to make this guide as accurate and useful as possible. However, many things can change after a guide is published—trails are rerouted, regulations change, facilities come under new management, etc.

We would love to hear from you concerning your experiences with this guide and how you feel it could be improved and kept up to date. While we may not be able to respond to all comments and suggestions, we'll take them to heart and we'll also make certain to share them with the author. Please send your comments and suggestions to the following address:

> The Globe Pequot Press
> Reader Response/Editorial Department
> P.O. Box 480
> Guilford, CT 06437

Or you may e-mail us at:

> editorial@GlobePequot.com

Thanks for your input, and happy trails!

Best Easy Day Hikes Series

Best Easy Day Hikes
Long Island

Susan Finch

FALCONGUIDES®

GUILFORD, CONNECTICUT
HELENA, MONTANA

AN IMPRINT OF THE GLOBE PEQUOT PRESS

FALCONGUIDES®

TOPO! Explorer software and SuperQuad source maps courtesy of National Geographic Maps. For information about TOPO! Explorer, TOPO!, and Nat Geo Maps products, go to www.topo.com or www.natgeomaps.com
Maps by Offroute Inc. © Morris Book Publishing LLC

Library of Congress Cataloging-in-Publication Data
Finch, Susan.
  Best easy day hikes, Long Island / Susan Finch.
     p. cm. – (Best easy day hikes series)
  ISBN 978-0-7627-5539-4
 1. Hiking–New York (State)–Long Island–Guidebooks. 2. Long Island (N.Y.)–Guidebooks. I. Title.
  GV199.42.N652L6638 2009
  917.47'210444–dc22

                                          2009022535

Printed in the United States of America

10 9 8 7 6 5 4 3 2 1

Contents

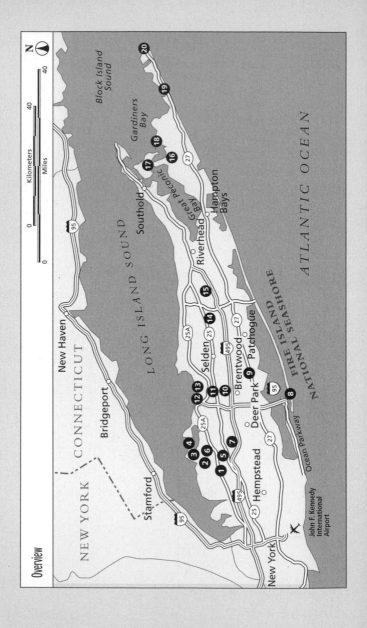

Acknowledgments

Thanks to my hiking partner, best friend, and husband, Drew Padrutt, for all his insight and ongoing support while trekking across Long Island. I can't think of anyone else I'd rather spend a day at work with. I owe another round of gratitude to Ron Finch for his unwavering standards of perfection and vast geographical knowledge; I couldn't have done it without you. Thanks to my mom, family, and friends for supporting me through another quest of finding the best trails. And a big thank you to Julie Hill, the New York State parks, preserve, and wildlife system, and the staff at FalconGuides, who shared their knowledge and expertise for this book.

Introduction

Long Island's trails offer a startling mix of terrain, from shoreline excursions to ocean-side bluffs to towering white pines and woodland forests, often all existing within a single park. Hike to the seal hangout at Montauk Point before heading uphill through a hardwood forest to search for the legendary bounty at Money Pond. Or explore the rare plant species of Mashomack Preserve and the phantom forest of the ever-shifting Walking Dunes. Wherever you hike, Long Island's trails are without the generic familiarity that comes from knowing a region inside and out. Each hike feels like a fresh adventure waiting to tell its own timeless story and stamped by an inspired signature of history, mystery, beauty, or tranquility.

Hitting the trails and supporting Long Island's park, preserve, and wildlife refuge system is also a much-needed reminder of what lies beyond the tangle of suburban civilization. Just beyond the borders of Middle Island's residential blanket, at Prosser Pines Preserve, rests one of the country's last pine forest plantations. A king's ruins lay deep in the woods alongside Muttontown's trails, and Walt Whitman's inspired steps can be retraced to the highest point on Long Island.

And the region doesn't come without opportunity for a beachside excursion. Water views that stretch beyond the reach of highways and roads can be explored on foot and lead to a handful of towering bluffs and historic lighthouses just waiting to be rediscovered.

It's nearly impossible to settle on just twenty hikes worthy of a Best Easy Day Hikes title, but these chapters are just

1

a hopeful handful of what each region can offer an aspiring day hiker. Whether you're just visiting or call it home, Long Island's contours will continue to surprise.

The Nature of Long Island

Long Island's hikes range from flat strolls along tall white pines to rugged bluffs overlooking the Long Island Sound. Hikers can find a variety of hikes that are easy to moderate in difficultly, with options for more challenging hikes. Long Island is home to a variety of endangered plants and wildlife species, some of which are found nowhere else on earth.

Weather

Long Island's weather resembles much of the Northeast region, with cold snowy winters blanketed with ice, humid summers, and temperate springs and autumns scattered with rain.

Snow and ice don't have to be deterrents to hiking, provided you choose flat terrain free of potentially icy pavement and slippery hills. Frozen ground can actually provide a protective sheath from mud and snow-kissed trails. Keep in mind that weather conditions can vary from one fork of Long Island to the other. A mild winter day on the western tip of the island may be mirrored with a frigid day on the eastern tip. Traveling toward Fire Island or the shores of Long Island will generally result in a good 10-degree drop from the inland terrain.

Summer days are typically hot and humid, with more relief near the edges of Long Island's shores. Dehydration and sunburn are typical warm-weather dangers, as are mosquitoes and biting insects. But traffic may be your worst obstacle, as a Saturday trip to the Hamptons in July could take twice as long as one on an early spring morning.

The rainy season edges in from March through May and unexpected downpours are frequent. It's best to bring a dry change of clothes and shoes after a long day on the trails. Remember that hikes surrounding the coast and along hilly terrain will require heavy boots after a rain. Mud is commonplace and is slow to dry under the forest cover of thick hardwoods. When chilly and damp, don't forget to drink plenty of water while hiking and adjust your trip time for difficult footing and traffic.

Be Prepared

Long Island's parks, preserves, and wildlife refuges are generally safe and easy to maneuver. However, this book is never an alternative to commonsense safety and preparation. Here are some tips to consider:

- Bring along a first-aid kit and have a basic knowledge of treating insect bites, wounds, and sprains.
- Drink plenty of water and wear adequate sunscreen, even during winter months.
- Bring a hiking buddy with you, or tell someone where you're going and how long you'll be gone.
- Avoid hiking to isolated bluffs, rocks, overlooks, and rims.
- Do not approach or feed wildlife including harbor seals, water fowl, and forest animals. You might disrupt their nesting and eating habits and create an association to humans with food.

- Do not drink from rivers, harbors, or streams without an adequate water filter that can remove harmful bacteria. It's best to carry your own water.
- Dress in layers and bring along a clean pair of shoes, socks, and a sweatshirt in case of rain or snow.
- Stay on marked trails at all times and obey the trail's reminder fences and trespassing signs.
- Make note of the time and always return to your car before the trail closes.

Zero Impact

Trails and footpaths throughout Long Island are used heavily year-round, especially during summer tourist season. To help protect and preserve our trails, here are a few tips to keep in mind:

- Pack out all your own trash, including biodegradable items like orange peels. You might also dispose of garbage left by less considerate hikers.
- Don't approach or feed any wild creatures—the ground squirrel eyeing your snack food is best able to survive if it remains self-reliant.
- Don't pick wildflowers and leaves or gather rocks, antlers, feathers, and other treasures along the trail. Removing these items will only take away from the next hiker's experience.
- Avoid damaging trailside soils and plants by remaining on the established route. This is also a good rule of thumb for avoiding poison oak and stinging nettle, common regional trailside irritants.
- Don't cut switchbacks—this can promote erosion.

- Be courteous by not making loud noises while hiking.
- Many of these trails are multiuse, which means you'll share them with other hikers, trail runners, mountain bikers, and equestrians. Familiarize yourself with proper trail etiquette, yielding the trail when appropriate.
- Use outhouses at trailheads or along the trail.

Long Island Boundaries

The day hikes included in this guide stretch from western to eastern Long Island and do not include Brooklyn or Queens. Almost every hike is accessible from the Long Island Expressway (I-495) and can be found by using the trailhead directions in each chapter.

Land Management

The following government and private organizations manage most of the public lands described in this guide, and can provide further information on these hikes and other trails in their service areas:

- Suffolk County Department of Parks, (631) 854-4423, www.suffolkcountyny.gov
- Nassau County Department of Parks, Recreation, and Museums, (516) 571-8500, www.nassaucountyny.gov
- U.S. Fish and Wildlife Refuge, Long Island National Wildlife Refuge Complex, 360 Smith Road, P.O. Box 21, Shirley, NY 11967, (631) 286-0485, www.fws.gov
- The Nature Conservancy in New York, 4245 North Fairfax Drive, Suite 100, Arlington, VA 22203, (703) 841-5300, www.nature.org

- New York State Office of Parks, Recreation and Historic Preservation, Empire State Plaza, Agency Building 1, Albany, NY 12238, (518) 474-0456, www.nysparks.state.ny.us
- Long Island Greenbelt Trail Conference, P.O. Box 5636, Hauppauge, NY, 11788-0141, (631) 360-0753, www.hike-LIGreenbelt.com

Public Transportation

The Long Island Railroad offers limited transportation options to area parks. However, all require a bus transfer or taxi to get from the train station to the parks, preserves, and wildlife refuges. Never attempt to hike from a station to the trails, as sidewalks are scarce and heavy traffic abounds.

How to Use This Book

This guide is designed to be simple and easy to use. Each hike is illustrated with a map and described by summary information that delivers the trail's vital statistics including length, difficulty, park hours, canine compatibility, and trail contacts. Directions to the trailhead are also provided, along with a general description of what you'll see along the way. A detailed route finder (Miles and Directions) sets forth mileages between significant landmarks along the trail.

Hike Selection

This guide describes trails that are accessible to every hiker, whether a visitor from out of town or someone lucky enough to live on Long Island. The hikes are no longer than 5.5 miles round-trip, and some are considerably shorter. They range in difficulty from flat excursions perfect for a family outing to more challenging treks in the bluffs along the Long Island Sound. While these trails are among the best, keep in mind that nearby trails, often in the same park or preserve, may offer options better suited to your needs. The hikes are generally arranged starting from west to east, so you can find more than one day hike in each area.

Difficulty Ratings

The hikes in this book are relatively easy even for a novice, with the exception of some hills and difficult footing. To aid in the selection of a hike that suits particular needs and abilities, each hike is rated either easy or moderate. Bear in mind that the more challenging routes can be made easy by hiking within your limits and taking rests when you need them.

- **Easy** hikes are generally short and flat and take no longer than an hour to complete.
- **Moderate** hikes involve increased distance and relatively mild changes in elevation, and will take one to two hours to complete.

The ratings are based on individual experience, and your own opinion may differ depending on your overall endurance and hiking enjoyment.

Approximate hiking times are based on the assumption that on flat ground, most walkers average 2.0 miles per hour. Adjust that rate by the steepness of the terrain and your level of fitness (subtract time if you're an aerobic animal and add time if you're hiking with kids), and you have a ballpark hiking duration. Be sure to add more time if you plan to picnic or take part in other activities like birdwatching or photography.

Trail Finder

Best Hikes for River Lovers

Best Hikes for Lake Lovers

Best Hikes for Children

Best Hikes for Dogs

Best Hikes for Great Views

Best Hikes for Nature Lovers

Best Hikes for History Buffs

Map Legend

═══〈95〉═══	Interstate Highway
═══〈27〉═══	State Highway
======	Unpaved Roads
───────	Local Roads
▬▬▬▬▬▬	Featured Trail
---------	Trail
〜〜〜	River/Creek
⬭	Ocean/Lake/Pond
ⅢⅢⅢ	Boardwalk/Steps
‿	Bridge
▲	Camping
🅿	Parking
■	Point of Interest/Structure
🚻	Restroom
○	Town
⓫	Trailhead
🔲	Viewpoint/Overlook
❓	Visitor/Information Center

1 Muttontown Trail

Loop through the mysterious trails of Muttontown Preserve to uncover aging ruins, hidden treasure, a walled garden, and rolling, open fields on some 550 acres of preserve.

Distance: 3.0-mile loop
Approximate hike time: 2½ hours
Difficulty: Moderate due to numerous side trails and tricky map navigation
Trail surface: Grass, gravel, dirt, and paved
Best season: Apr through Oct

Other trail users: Equestrians
Canine compatibility: Leashed dogs permitted
Schedule: Open daily from 9:00 a.m. to 4:30 p.m.
Maps: USGS quad: Hicksville
Contact: Muttontown Preserve, East Norwich; (516) 571-8500; www.nassaucountyny.gov

Finding the trailhead: Take the Long Island Expressway (I-495) to exit 41 and head north on Route 106. Continue for 4.1 miles to the intersection with Route 25A / Northern Boulevard. Turn left and drive for 0.1 mile and left again onto Muttontown Lane. Drive through two stop signs to the preserve entrance and make a quick jaunt to the left to the parking area. Walk around the Nature Center adjacent to the parking lot to locate maps and the trailhead. GPS: N40 50.17' / W73 32.4'

The Hike

While eclectic mansions, open fields, and tranquil ponds brush up against a forest of Japanese red maple and oak, the stunning preserve also holds secrets of lost bounty, murder, and mystery. Folklore surrounds the Knollwood estate, an ominous sixty-room granite palace built in the early 1900s by Charles Hudson. The estate was purchased in 1951 by

Ahmed Bey Zogu, president of Albania from 1925 to 1928. Zogu proclaimed himself king just a few years into his term and became known as King Zog. After discovering the Knollwood estate, Zog allegedly purchased it with rubies and diamonds for a tidy sum of over $100,000. Treasure hunters later vandalized the grounds, believing the king's loot was underfoot.

But the ground's history isn't just the stuff of royalty and lost bounty. It also contains a puzzling murder mystery. As recently as 2001, a group of men found a piece of bone sticking through forest cover that lead to a skeleton lying in the fetal position. The case remains unsolved to date. Is there more than just treasure lingering among the ruins of Knollwood?

To find out, start your hike adjacent to the Nature Center just off the parking lot. Walk behind the center to locate restrooms, maps, and two trailheads. Take the dirt trail leading to the left and follow the yellow trail blazes.

Keep hiking past the chain-link fence and turn left at the first fork, followed by a right at the next intersection. Keep straight until you reach a wide fork that makes a T formation, then make a right followed by another quick right. Blue penstemon, wild violet, and mayapple line the paths and peer through discarded leaves. You might discover shrews, red foxes, raccoons, or moles rummaging in the forest cover.

Continue hiking and bear left at 0.3 mile at a wooden hiking post. Next, hang a left at the fork at 0.5 mile, continue straight, and walk into a grassy field, listening for bluebirds and the light hum of traffic from the road on your left. At 0.7 mile take a right at the fork and bear right again to access the spur trail to cut through the grassy field. Tall weeds surround you and take you through the thick of the trail.

When you exit look straight ahead for the equestrian area and wooden fences and continue straight. Walk past the information kiosk and turn right at 1.1 miles to continue into the woods along a wide dirt corridor.

When you reach 1.3 miles, turn left at the fork and venture into the winding swatch of woods, home to apple trees, rhododendrons, and fingers of delicate ivy. Keep left at the four-way intersection and then right at the upcoming fork and make your way to the lavish columns of King Zog's infamous ruins. By now you should notice Muttontown's blend of tranquil woodlands, quiet trails, and often eerie atmosphere.

Walk directly into the ruins until you reach the ornate wall in the back and race up the steps just on your right. From here, admire the views of the preserve underfoot, imagining King Zog's elaborate plans for his retirement and faithful subjects. Bear left and continue to the four-way intersection, followed by another left, and take the middle path down to the walled gardens.

Keeping the garden to your left, follow along the garden wall and bear right at its end, followed by a quick left. Turn right at the hiking post, then left when you reach the wide dirt trail, and left again at the T-shaped intersection. Pass through a dogwood field and then make a right and pass by the chain-link fence from the start of your hike. Make a left at the wide T and keep leaning left at the next fork. From here, follow your original path back to the Nature Center entrance to complete your mystery hike.

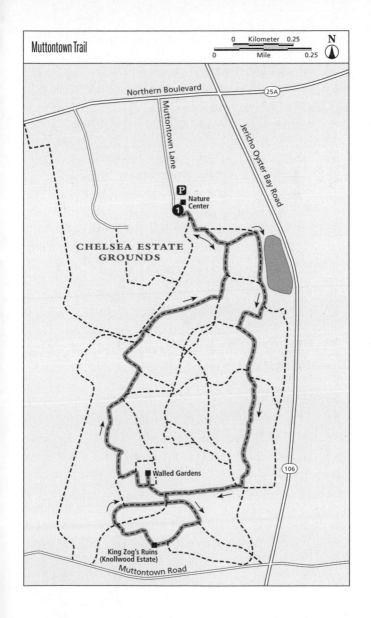

Muttontown Trail

Northern Boulevard 25A

Muttontown Lane

Jericho Oyster Bay Road

P

1 Nature Center

CHELSEA ESTATE GROUNDS

106

Walled Gardens

King Zog's Ruins
(Knollwood Estate)

Muttontown Road

0   Kilometer 0.25

0   Mile   0.25

N

Miles and Directions

0.0 Start at the back of the Nature Center.

0.2 Turn right and keep bearing right at the upcoming fork. Walk along the fence on your left.

0.3 Bear left at the hiking post to walk the loop clockwise.

0.5 Turn left at the fork.

0.7 Turn right at the fork and bear right again to access the spur trail cutting directly into the meadow.

1.1 Walk past the information kiosk and turn right onto a wide dirt path.

1.3 Turn left at the fork and hike into the woods. Then turn left at the four-way intersection, then right at the upcoming fork.

1.4 Stop to view the ruins. Walk up the stairs at the back wall of the ruins and veer left.

1.7 Return to the four-way intersection and turn left followed by another left. Take the middle path with the Walled Gardens on your left.

1.8 Stop to see the Walled Gardens. Turn right at the end of the wall.

2.0 Bear left.

2.2 Bear left again, taking a right at the next fork.

2.5 Turn left and continue hiking straight.

2.7 Turn left and backtrack to the Nature Center.

3.0 End at the Nature Center.

2 Sagamore Hill

Pay a visit to the former home of Teddy Roosevelt. Follow in his historic footsteps to a harbor-side boardwalk and take a stroll through the historic grounds.

Distance: 2.0-mile loop
Approximate hike time: 1½ hours
Difficulty: Easy
Trail surface: Pavement, boardwalk, and sand
Best season: Apr through Oct
Other trail users: History buffs

Canine compatibility: Leashed dogs permitted
Schedule: Dawn until dusk, year-round
Maps: USGS quad: Lloyd Harbor
Contact: National Park Service, U.S. Department of the Interior, Oyster Bay; (516) 922-4788; www.nps.gov/sahi

Finding the trailhead: Take the Long Island Expressway (I-495) to exit 41N and continue on Route 106 north for 4.0 miles. Turn right and head east on Route 25A for 2.5 miles. At the third traffic light, turn left and continue northwest on Cove Road for 1.7 miles. At Cove Neck Road turn right and drive 1.5 miles to the Sagamore Hill entrance on your right. GPS: N40 53.10' / W73 29.58'

The Hike

Theodore Roosevelt resided on the quiet, wooded grounds of Sagamore Hill from 1885 until his death in 1919. The area was named for the Indian chief Sagamore Mohannis. Dubbed the country's first "Summer White House," the grounds feature eighty acres of manicured grounds, sloping terrain, thick forest, the Old Orchard Museum, and a half-mile wooded loop trail to Cold Spring Harbor.

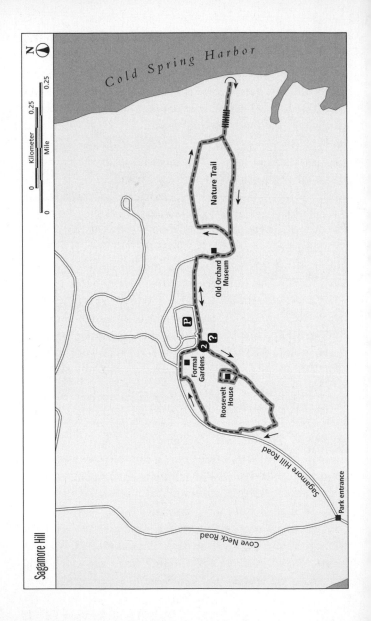

Sagamore Hill

Cold Spring Harbor

N

0   Kilometer   0.25

0   Mile   0.25

Nature Trail

Old Orchard Museum

P

Formal Gardens

2

?

Roosevelt House

Sagamore Hill Road

Cove Neck Road

Park entrance

Built between 1884 and 1885, the ornate twenty-three-room Queen Anne–style home is the crowning jewel of the grounds and was said to be Roosevelt's dream home. In 1901 Roosevelt began his first term as president of the United States and hosted conferences and negotiated events at his summer home. The relatively unchanged home features paintings, flags, and weapons from his tenure.

To retrace the steps of Roosevelt himself, start your hike just left of the visitor center after grabbing a map from one of the kiosks near the door. Lean right and walk behind the center to explore the informational plaques about the former toolshed, carriage house, and stables that once stood on the grounds. Next, head toward the oversized windmill watching over Roosevelt's former home and make your way to the front porch of the stately building. Plan in advance to spend an extra hour or two on a tour of the home—call ahead for current schedules and wait times. After getting to know more about the Roosevelts, continue walking along the paved path, veer right onto a wooded path, and walk downhill to see where Teddy's tennis courts and pet cemetery once lay.

Keep walking along the dirt and pine straw–covered path back toward the visitor center. From here, you can follow signs to the Old Orchard Museum, leading through an open field and to the Orchard House. To find the trailhead to the Nature Path, a side trail, walk behind the museum and look for the hiking emblem and a wooded trail sloping downhill. Take a left at the upcoming fork, and as you hike down to the harbor, consider these were the same steps the president once took on his beloved strolls to Cold Spring Harbor.

In all, the grounds cover eighty-three acres of forest, meadows, salt marsh, and beach with a variety of birds, turtles, and insects roaming the grounds. When you reach the fork to the wooden boardwalk, turn left and walk over Eel Creek and down to the beach. Once you've had your fill of water views, return to the fork you came from and continue left to complete your loop. Walk back uphill and stop to visit the Orchard House before returning to the visitor center where you started the hike.

Miles and Directions

0.0 As you start, bear right behind the visitor center.

0.1 Turn toward the windmill.

0.2 Loop around Roosevelt House.

0.3 Bear right onto the wooded trail and slope downhill.

0.4 Walk on the path parallel to the street.

0.5 Bear right.

0.6 Turn right and walk toward the parking area.

0.7 Follow the signs to the museum.

0.9 Turn right and walk behind the museum to pick up the nature trail.

1.0 Bear left at the fork.

1.2 Turn left onto the boardwalk, cross over Eel Creek, and explore the beach.

1.5 Backtrack to the boardwalk and turn left.

1.8 Pass the museum and walk back to the parking area.

2.0 End the hike back at the visitor center.

3 Caumsett State Park

Explore the former grounds of a department-store magnate to see a working dairy farm, freshwater pond, hardwood forest, and secluded views of the Long Island Sound.

Distance: 4.1-mile loop
Approximate hike time: 3½ hours
Difficulty: Moderate due to some hills
Trail surface: Paved, dirt, and sand
Best season: May through Oct
Other trail users: Fishermen, hunters, and scientists

Canine compatibility: Dogs not permitted
Schedule: Sunrise to sunset, year-round
Maps: USGS quad: Lloyd Harbor
Contact: New York State Office of Parks, Recreation and Historic Preservation, Huntington; (631) 423-1770; http://nysparks .state.ny.us

Finding the trailhead: Take the Long Island Expressway (I-495) east to exit 49 and continue on Route 110 north to Huntington. Turn right onto Route 25A/Main Street. Turn left (north) onto West Neck Road, which becomes Lloyd Harbor Road in approximately 2 miles. Turn left into the park and park next to the main entrance. GPS: N40 55.4' / W73 28.21'

The Hike

In 1921 Marshal Field III, grandson of the department-store magnate, bought 1,750 acres in Lloyd Neck and named it Caumsett. This Matinecock Indian name means "place by a sharp rock" as a nod to its home on a rocky peninsula extending into the Long Island Sound. Field turned it into an expansive hunting preserve and country club featuring

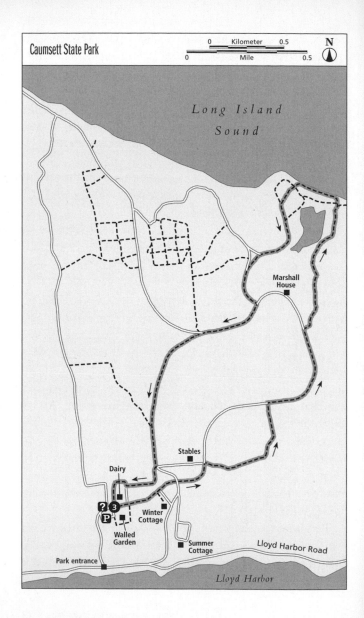

Caumsett State Park

Kilometer
0   0.5
Mile
0   0.5

N

Long Island Sound

Marshall House

Stables

Dairy

❓ **3**

🅿

Winter Cottage

Walled Garden

Summer Cottage

Lloyd Harbor Road

Park entrance

Lloyd Harbor

nearly every sport imaginable except golf. The grounds were designed for self-sufficiency, complete with award-winning cattle, vegetables, its own water and power supplies, and a Tudor-style manor. The state of New York acquired the land in 1961 and opened it to the public for fishing, bird-watching, biking, horseback riding, nature study, and hiking. It also contains a dairy, nature trails, a rocky shoreline, and a salt marsh.

Start hiking past the visitor center, keeping the dairy complex on your left. Just before a four-way intersection, look for the Winter Cottage on your right. Despite its quaint name, its size could rival a modern-day Long Island mansion. Keep straight at the fork and continue until you arrive at the riding stables and see a spur trail just on your right. Walk down into the forest of hardwoods and look for gray foxes and songbirds as you pass by open fields sprinkled with wildflowers and dirt paths leading to residential homes. You might also spot garlic mustard, black birch, and chokeberry along the trail. Keep left at the next several intersections and continue uphill.

When you reach the paved road again, turn right and continue as it bends left and then straightens out. At 1.4 miles turn right toward the residential home tucked away on a slight decline. Stick to the left and cross under the power lines to pick up the trail leading back into the woods. Keep to your left at the next fork and walk into an open meadow, then bear right and walk along the freshwater fishing pond.

Pass through the corridor of maples and cedars until views of the shore and Long Island Sound open up at the north end. Skip off the path down to the beach and turn left to enjoy the water's edge. When you see the trail open back up to the beach to head inland at 2.2 miles, turn left at the large oaks and walk along the west end of the pond. Keep right at the upcoming series of forks until you emerge on the paved road once again. Turn right and enjoy a leisurely stroll back by following signs for 1.3 miles to the main entrance. When you see the dairy complex, turn right at the fork and wind around the buildings for a view of the staff hard at work. Return to the main entrance and parking lot, stopping in the visitor center to learn more about Caumsett's history and wildlife.

Miles and Directions

0.0 Start the hike adjacent to visitor center.

0.3 Walk through the four-way intersection.

0.5 Walk toward the stables and turn right at the dirt path leading down into woods.

0.7 Keep left and straight at the fork next to the residential area.

1.0 Return to the paved road and turn right.

1.4 Turn right into the driveway of the residence and keep left. Locate the new trail just past the power lines and keep left at the fork.

1.8 Pass by a freshwater pond on your left.

2.0 Walk onto the beach and turn left.

2.2 Return to the trail on your left.

2.8 Turn right at the paved path and follow the signs back to the main entrance.

3.8 Turn right to wind around the dairy complex and follow the exit signs to the main entrance.

4.1 End the hike adjacent to visitor center.

4 Target Rock National Wildlife Refuge

Take a hike down to the beach and learn more about this refuge's thriving birding community. Catch a glimpse of lounging harbor seals and learn about the historic namesake of Target Rock.

Distance: 1.5-mile loop
Approximate hike time: 1 hour
Difficulty: Easy
Trail surface: Dirt, rock, sand, and paved
Best season: Year-round to see varied wildlife
Other trail users: None
Canine compatibility: Dogs not permitted

Schedule: Open ½ hour before sunset to ½ hour after sunset, year-round
Maps: USGS quad: Lloyd Harbor
Contact: Long Island National Wildlife Refuge Complex, Huntington; (631) 286-0485.; www .fws.gov/refuges/profiles/index .cfm?id=52568

Finding the trailhead: From Huntington Village, take Route 25A through Main Street. Turn north onto West Neck Road for 5.0 miles and continue driving as it changes to Lloyd Neck Road for approximately 7.4 miles. When the road turns into Target Rock Road, drive for approximately 0.5 mile and look for the entrance on the right. Park your car near the restrooms and locate the well-marked trailhead by the map kiosk. GPS: N40 55.38' / W73 26.17'

The Hike

Legend suggests Target Rock National Wildlife Refuge got its name during the Revolutionary War and War of 1812 when British soldiers used a large rock jutting out over Huntington Bay as target practice. The area later became

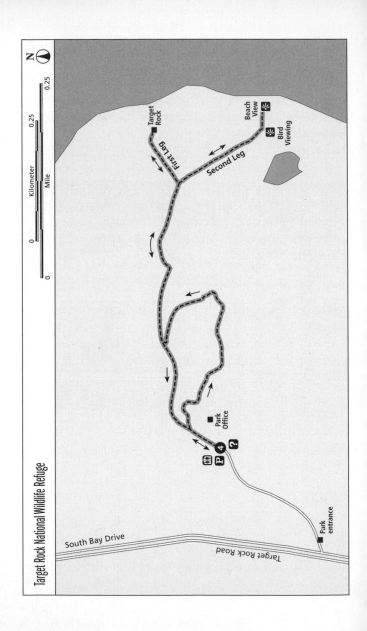

Target Rock National Wildlife Refuge

known as Target Rock Farm and was eventually owned by investment banker Ferdinand Eberstadt in 1927, who helped shape its ongoing preservation efforts. During his tenure on the grounds, a thirty-five-room neo-Georgian mansion was constructed along with cultivated formal gardens on the grounds.

In 1967 Target Rock was donated to the federal government under the Migratory Bird Conservation Act in an effort to ensure its preservation. Today the eighty acres feature trails snaking through a forest of hardwood oaks and hickories with grape, catbrier, and blackberry shrubs spilling toward the trails. The refuge also boasts a salt marsh, vernal ponds, tidal waters, forest, and formal gardens with varied wildlife.

Start your journey by the information kiosk and lean right onto the gravel path. At 0.4 mile bear right and walk past homes on your left and through the forest. During your hike look for chestnut oaks housing neotropical songbirds including gray catbirds, house finches, American robin, rufous-sided towhee, northern oriole, and bank swallow.

At 0.7 mile turn left and walk to the observation deck at Target Rock looking out over the harbor. This is a prime spot to see the beach and surrounding towns of Long Island resting against the harbor. Two tidal flats in the bay house glacial erratics and blue mussel. The upland terrain is covered in beach grass or prone to bald spots with little to no vegetation.

Backtrack to the main trail and turn left once again, sloping down toward the beach. Pass by the brackish pond at around 0.9 mile and look for the viewing shelters to spot some of the resident waterfowl. You really can't pick a bad month to hike the refuge. If you're hiking around winter, from October through March, you might see puddle ducks, black ducks, goldeneye, and greater scaup, among others. In all, some 200 species of birds have been spotted throughout the preserve. If you look south, you might see a small outlet surrounded by marsh elder that connects the pond to the tide.

Stop at the beach and look for loafing harbor seals and leatherback turtles. Horned grebes, yellowlegs, semipalmated plover, spotted sandpiper, red-throated loons, and great cormorants commune near the water's edge.

After exploring the beach, return to the trail and backtrack. At 1.2 miles continue straight, returning to the trailhead. At miles 1.2 and 1.4, the trail you took out toward the beach will intersect from the left.

Miles and Directions

0.0 Start at the trailhead adjacent to the information kiosk.

0.4 Bear right, walk past the residential area, and take another right at the fork.

0.7 Turn left and walk to the observation deck overlooking the beach. Backtrack to the main trail and turn left, continuing straight to the beach.

0.9 Walk past the pond on your right and continue down to the beach. Backtrack to the main trail and continue straight.

1.2 Continue straight back to the trailhead. (**Option:** Take a hard left to retrace your steps back through the forest to return to the trailhead.)

1.5 End the hike back at the trailhead.

5 Stillwell Woods

Take it easy on a leisurely loop through tall grassy meadows and sloping forests.

Distance: 1.6-mile loop
Approximate hike time: 1 hour
Difficulty: Easy
Trail surface: Grass and dirt
Best season: Mar through Oct
Other trail users: None
Canine compatibility: Leashed dogs permitted

Schedule: Open daily from 7:00 a.m. to dark
Maps: USGS quad: Hicksville
Contact: Nassau County Department of Parks, Recreation, and Museums, Syosset; (516) 571-3000; www.nassaucountyny.gov

Finding the trailhead: Take the Long Island Expressway (I-495) to exit 44 for Route 135 north. Drive 1.0 mile and turn right onto Route 25 at Jericho Turnpike. Turn left onto South Woods Road and continue for another 1.3 miles. When you pass Syosset High School on your left, turn right into Stillwell Woods Park. Look for the trailhead at the end of the road near the maintenance road. GPS: N40 49.55' / W73 28.40'

The Hike

At first glance Stillwell Woods may look like little more than a grassy recreational haunt nestled next to a busy road near Syosset High School. Baseball fields and recreational areas abound along the borders of hidden hiking trails.

But upon closer examination, you might be surprised at what you find. Inside the wooded 270-acre preserve lies a lush community of oak barrens, bicycle and equestrian trails, sloping ravines, a patchwork of wildflowers, and bustling bird life. Much of the plant life and wildlife are more com-

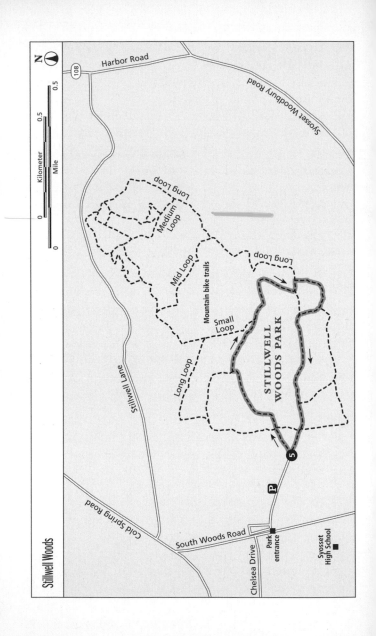

Stillwell Woods

mon to eastern Long Island and create a unique community right in Stillwell Woods. The preserve also offers a complex mix of easy to moderate trails with plenty of options to get lost in nature.

For a true easy day hike with leisure in mind, hikers can make a loop around the meadow area along the multiuse bike trail for a peek at the surrounding woods and expansive open fields. There's also plenty of opportunity to venture into the forest to gain access to a series of splintering uphill and winding trails, including the Suffolk Greenbelt Trail and Sierra Club Trail.

After parking at the end of the baseball field near the dirt maintenance road by the map kiosk, cut across the north end of the fields and look for a trailhead on your right. Begin your stroll, bear left, and hike until you see well-marked signs for the Stillwell Woods main loop. Skip past the signs directing you to the more difficult hike and glide through the open fields.

Keep hiking past the tall grasses shielding you from the suburban outcroppings of residential neighborhoods. You'll also notice splinters of oaks and laurels encroaching along the perimeters of the fields. Bring a pair of binoculars to watch a sprinkling of bird boxes and nests scattered through the fields.

At around 0.8 mile keep bearing right to hedge your way to the completion of a full-circuit loop. But if you want to venture into the woods and explore the oaks, red cedars, blueberry bushes, and mature hardwoods, proceed left and snake into the woods for a look at the sloping terrain and tangle of biking trails and a slice of the Suffolk Greenbelt Trail. Be careful not to venture too deep, as hikers often stumble up the hills into residential neighborhoods and lose that tranquil sense of wooded isolation and beauty of Stillwell Woods.

After taking a moment to appreciate the preserve, keep winding past the open fields, where you might find a rogue car or renegade ATV resting along the maintenance road, to enjoy a picnic or quick rest. This area is a good spot to stretch your legs and bring out a pair of binoculars to watch the influx of birding activity, which includes ring-necked pheasants. Around sunset you might even see a fury of cottontail rabbits making one last round for supper before dark.

Once you've had your fill of birding and wildlife, continue down the service road. You can either continue straight to meet up with your car or take a right at the last fork to end up at the trailhead you started from.

Miles and Directions

0.0 Start on the trail by turning left from the parking area near the maintenance road. Walk into the grass and look for the trailhead on your right.

0.3 Locate signs for the bike trail and continue following the signs around the loop.

0.8 Bear right and continue looping.

1.6 End the hike back at the trailhead.

6 Uplands Farm Sanctuary

Hike through grassy meadows to isolated upland woods on a ninety-seven-acre preserve.

Distance: 2.0-mile double loop
Approximate hike time: 1½ hours
Difficulty: Easy
Trail surface: Grass, dirt, and gravel
Best season: Apr through Oct
Other trail users: None

Canine compatibility: Dogs not permitted
Schedule: Open year-round from dawn until dusk
Maps: USGS quad: Huntington
Contact: The Uplands Farm Sanctuary, Cold Spring Harbor; (631) 367-3384; www.nature.org

Finding the trailhead: Take the Long Island Expressway (I-495) east to exit 48 north. Follow Round Swamp Road north to Jericho Turnpike/Route 25. Take a left on Jericho Turnpike and at the next traffic light, take a right onto Avery Road. Turn right onto Woodbury Road in 0.5 mile and then left onto Route 108 and follow it until it ends. Take a right up the hill to Lawrence Hill Road and look for the Nature Conservancy entrance on the right at the top of the hill. Drive in the entrance road to the parking lot. The trailhead is next to the kiosk. GPS: N40 51.27' / W73 27.11'

The Hike

The sight of Uplands Farm's wooden split-rail fences and a wrought-iron weathervane might conjure images of an old-fashioned farm right from the pages of a storybook. But behind its charming facade lies a rich history with an environmental impact. This ninety-seven-acre preserve was once owned by J. P. Morgan's daughter, Jane Nichols Page,

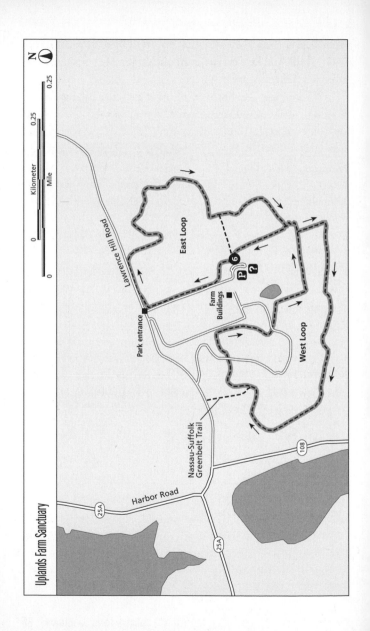

Uplands Farm Sanctuary

who donated part of the property to the Nature Conservancy in 1962 before the remaining acreage was donated after her death in the 1980s.

Hit the paths to discover an enticing loop hike weaving through rows of oak hedgerows, vernal pools, and upland woods that are home to more than forty species of butterflies and a thriving bird community. Pick up the trailhead adjacent to the Daniel P. Davidson Trail kiosk in front of the parking lot. Take an immediate left to hike along the open meadows and walk down toward the road you drove in from.

As you curve around the fields, take note that without meticulous mowing and care, the area would revert back to its original woodland state. The Nature Conservancy works diligently to maintain a diverse and open space that is quickly disappearing from Long Island. The fields are also home to a flurry of bird activity, from Baltimore orioles to red-winged blackbirds.

When you reach the fork at 0.4 mile, turn left and walk into the woods, looking for red maple, black cherry, hickory, and red cedar trees. Hikers should be able to catch sight of lilies of the valley and garlic mustard lined with maple trees. This brief detour will also wind through oak and ash trees before spilling back into the open meadow. Bear left and skip over the spur trails leading directly into the fields.

When you reach a fork near the homes at the loop's edge, glide left for a step or two and make a quick right, hiking up a gradual hill. Bear left up the hill, and after a mound of stones, lean right and walk downhill into the forest, where there's a scattering of oversized glacial erratics.

Continue right at the fork leading into the woods and look for oaks, tulip trees, and black birch with flowering dogwood while walking along a rim overlooking the ravines and the harbor. Pass the Nassau-Suffolk Greenbelt Trail, which veers left and leads a mile down to Cold Spring Harbor. Thickets of mountain laurel and maple leaf brush past as you hike back downhill toward the farm buildings. Shift right at the approaching fork and pick up the grassy edge of the western loop again and walk past the rail fence heading east. As you walk around private residences, the barn, and apple trees, you'll see the pond shifting into view. Continue walking around the western loop and head back to the parking lot where you started.

Miles and Direction

0.0 Start at the trailhead adjacent to the map kiosk.

0.4 Make a left and take a detour loop into the woods, bearing right.

0.7 Resurface in the grassy meadows and turn left.

0.9 Walk left for a few steps and take an immediate right up a slight hill.

1.1 Bear right and walk downhill through the woods.

1.3 Bear right and walk uphill, passing the trail to Cold Spring Harbor approaching from your left.

1.7 Wind right and walk downhill toward the farm buildings.

2.0 End back at the parking lot.

7 Walt Whitman Loop

Take a hike fit for a poet and see the highest point on Long Island, Jayne's Hill.

Distance: 4.1-mile loop
Approximate hike time: 3 hours
Difficulty: Moderate due to some hills
Trail surface: Dirt and gravel
Best season: Apr through Oct
Other trail users: Joggers and equestrians
Canine compatibility: Leashed dogs permitted
Schedule: Dawn until dusk, year-round
Maps: USGS quad: Huntington
Contact: West Hills County Park, Huntington; (631) 854-4423; www.suffolkcountyny.gov

Finding the trailhead: Take the Long Island Expressway (I-495) east to exit 42 and merge onto Northern State Parkway heading east. Exit at 40S and drive 0.25 mile south on Walt Whitman Road/Route 110. Take a right onto Old Country Road and drive for 0.3 mile. Turn right again on Sweet Hollow Road and drive for 0.5 mile to the parking lot on your right. Look for the trailhead at the edge of the woods by the playground. GPS: N40 48.5' / W73 25.16'

The Hike

Walt Whitman deemed the rolling hills and forested blanket of present-day West Hills County Park "romantic" and "beautiful" and was known to walk its trails with vigor. See the poetic inspiration for yourself with a walk amongst white pines and mountain laurels to the highest point on Long Island, Jayne's Hill. Resting at an elevation of just over 400 feet, the hill is nestled within a mixed deciduous forest covered in moccasin flower and ferns.

Start your hike by the edge of the woods near the playground area and venture into the wooded corridor. Bear right along the open field and then keep left and look for white blazes along the oak trees. When you pass a fence, watch for blue markings and turn left on the bridle trail followed by a right at the fork and another right. Cross over a handful of rambling spur trails, then left again at the upcoming sand-strewn path. Watch for horses and their well-placed greetings, as you're now hiking along a popular bridle path.

Lean to the left of a residential home and continue straight on the horse trail before turning left at an upcoming fork. Make another left and leave suburbia behind while continuing with the blue blazes. Make a quick right, walking along a ridge, and enjoy the company of aging mountain laurels as you bear right and make your way past a stable and steps made of wood and dirt.

Look for the white blazes just across the paved road and glide past a chain-link fence. Venture to your right at the upcoming fork, crossing over an unblazed trail. Slow down to admire the canopy of birch trees and follow the white blazes to the left at the next fork.

Let the banks of Toad Pond lull you over and continue following the white blazes while making your way steadily uphill. Turn left at another bridle trail and enter the parking lot to Jayne's Hill. From here, just keep to your right and follow along with the white blazes, enjoying the embrace of flowering dogwoods and black birch trees. Turn right at a playground area down a wide path, followed by a right and then a left. Watch as Jayne's Hill comes into view and stop to read the rock with a plaque honoring the late Whitman on his beloved hill.

Jayne's Hill, once called High Hill, was originally surveyed at 354 feet above sea level in 1825 by historian Silas Wood. It was later renamed for the Jayne family that lived in the area. The hill is a well-traveled spot and well worth the burst uphill through potentially muddy banks and trails.

Continue hiking past the rock and keep right as you make your way downhill through a patch of chokeberry while looking out for fingers of poison ivy tumbling over the trail. Pass by the fence, make a right onto the horse path, and follow the white blazes to your left at the upcoming fork. Hike straight through another junction and then turn left at the next fork to continue following the white blazes. Another right at the next turn will take you along a forested ridge with gently sloping views.

From here, keep following along with the white blazes to your left and cross over another bridle path and past a fence, where you will spot the silhouette of the stables just ahead. At the upcoming horse trail, turn left and then right before continuing straight over approaching trails, making your way to familiar ground. Keep walking until you see the playground and parking lot where you started.

Miles and Directions

0.0 Start your hike from the edge of the woods near the playground.

0.1 Keep right at the open field and follow the white blazes. Watch for upcoming blue blazes and bear left at the fence.

0.4 Turn left.

0.5 Bear right.

0.7 Wind right at fork.

0.9 Cross over an intersection and bend left.

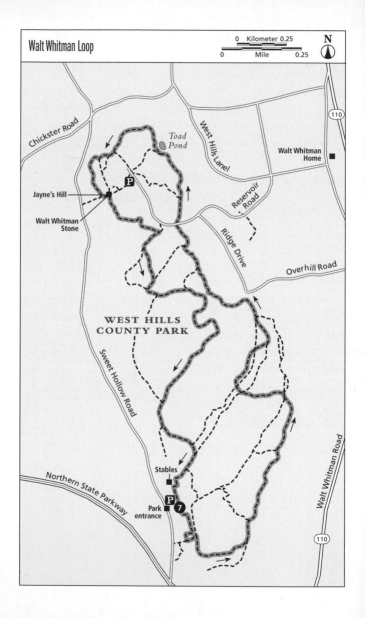

Walt Whitman Loop

0 Kilometer 0.25
0 Mile 0.25

N

Chickster Road

Toad Pond

West Hills Lanel

110

Walt Whitman Home

P

Jayne's Hill

Walt Whitman Stone

Reservoir Road

Ridge Drive

Overhill Road

WEST HILLS
COUNTY PARK

Sweet Hollow Road

Walt Whitman Road

Stables

Northern State Parkway

P 7

Park entrance

110

1.1 Go straight through the fork and wind right.

1.3 Proceed straight through an intersection and bend left.

1.4 Keep left.

1.6 Veer right.

1.7 Proceed straight through the upcoming intersections.

2.0 Bear right.

2.1 Keep right at the fork, then wind left.

2.3 Keep right around the parking lot.

2.6 Explore Jayne's Hill.

2.8 Keep right.

3.0 Continue right and straight.

3.2 Keep right.

3.7 Bear left.

3.9 Keep right.

4.1 End back at the playground area.

8 Fire Island Lighthouse

Hike to the legendary lighthouse on Fire Island and explore a nature trail, visit resident deer, and take an ocean–side stroll.

Distance: 1.9-mile loop
Approximate hike time: 1½ hours
Difficulty: Easy
Trail surface: Boardwalk, sand
Best season: Apr through Oct
Other trail users: None
Canine compatibility: Dogs not permitted

Schedule: Dawn until dusk, year-round
Maps: USGS quad: Bay Shore East
Contact: National Park Services, U.S. Department of the Interior, Fire Island; (631) 321-7028; www.nps.gov/fiis

Finding the trailhead: From the Long Island Expressway (I-495), take exit 53S to Sagtikos Parkway. Continue following signs for FINS, which are marked with a picture of a lighthouse. Just over the bridge at the old Robert Moses water tower, continue east and park in Field #5 just off the beach. GPS: N40 37.40' / W73 13.55'

The Hike

Fire Island served as a nautical center long before Long Island was ever colonized. Native Americans used the area for hunting and fishing before white settlers developed a thriving whaling industry. The iconic Fire Island Lighthouse was completed in 1858 to replace the 89-foot tower built in 1827. The light of the current tower stands 167 feet tall and was eventually decommissioned in 1974 by the U.S. Coast Guard. In the 1980s the Fire Island Lighthouse Preservation Society formed to preserve and restore both the tower and light, which today is still used for private navigation.

Start your hike on the boardwalk adjacent to the entrance and beachside restrooms at Parking Field #5 and enjoy hypnotic ocean views on your right. When you reach the pavement, look up and to your right for the start of the official boardwalk Nature Trail. Stop to read about the sandy dunes and the park's monarch butterfly, eastern cottontail, and red fox community. Deer are also popular along the boardwalk and it's not unusual to see a group of does within reach. Fire Island strongly discourages the petting or feeding of wildlife and works to preserve its vegetation and delicate dunes with controlled deer-bait traps scattered around the lighthouse.

Cross over a dirt road and hike past the fork on your left. At 0.8 mile ignore the fork in the boardwalk jutting right and make your way straight to the lighthouse. Stop inside to read about the history of the lighthouse and take a tour to see sparkling ocean views from the top. When you're finished, exit the visitor center doors and continue straight down the steps, over the dirt road, and to the boardwalk winding down to the beach.

When you reach the end of the boardwalk, turn right on the beach at 1.0 mile and make your way down the sandy shore back to the parking lot where you started.

But there's more to do on Fire Island than just lighthouse exploration. Hike through the nearly 300-year-old maritime forest, with its sassafras, black gum, and American holly, at Sunken Forest. For advanced hikers, consider the 1,363-acre Otis Pike Fire Island High Dune Wilderness, which boasts the only federally designated wilderness area in New York. This one-way, 7.0-mile hike features a trek through the barrier island ecosystem and coastal wilderness. Both areas are farther east along Fire Island.

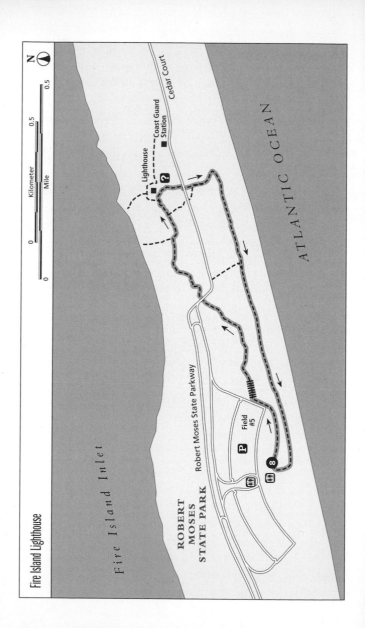

Fire Island Lighthouse

Fire Island Inlet

ROBERT MOSES STATE PARK

Robert Moses State Parkway

Field #5

Lighthouse

Coast Guard Station

Cedar Court

ATLANTIC OCEAN

N

0 0.5 Kilometer

0 0.5 Mile

Miles and Directions

0.0 Start at the restroom and recreational building at Parking Field #5 and walk onto the boardwalk.

0.2 Leave the beach boardwalk and veer left and pick up the Nature Trail boardwalk on your right.

0.5 Cross over the dirt road.

0.7 Pass by the fork on your left.

0.8 Pass the fork on your right and continue straight.

0.9 Explore the lighthouse.

1.0 Walk across the dirt road from the lighthouse visitor center, down the boardwalk, and turn right on the beach.

1.9 End the hike back at Parking Field #5.

9 Connetquot River State Park Preserve

Named for the Connetquot River, Long Island's largest state park boasts 3,473 acres of land and water and houses bird sanctuaries and an educational fishing hatchery. Stop at the old Grist Mill, walk by a pond full of wood duck and geese, and get to know the resident white-tailed deer nosing for a meal just off the trails.

Distance: 3.0-mile loop
Approximate hike time: 2½ hours
Difficulty: Easy
Trail surface: Gravel and dirt
Best season: Apr through Nov
Other trail users: Anglers
Canine compatibility: Dogs not permitted
Schedule: Open Apr through Sept Tues through Sun from 6:00 a.m. to 4:30 p.m. Open Oct through Mar Wed through Sun from 8:00 a.m. to 4:30 p.m.
Maps: USGS quad: Bay Shore East
Contact: Connetquot River State Park Preserve, Oakdale; (631) 581-1005; http://nysparks.state .ny.us

Finding the trailhead: Take Southern State Parkway east to exit 44 and proceed east on Route 27/Sunrise Highway for approximately 1.9 miles to Pond Road at exit 47A. When you reach the end of the ramp, turn left and use the overpass to cross over the highway and get in the westbound lane. After 1.4 miles turn right into the preserve and park by the tollbooth. GPS: N40 45.0' / W73 8.58'

The Hike

Wildlife lovers will appreciate this beautiful preserve and its fascinating residents. White-tailed deer are numerous throughout the preserve, as are snowy egret, great blue heron, and black-crowned night heron looking for a bite of fresh trout.

For nearly a century, Connetquot State Park was the stomping grounds of a hundred wealthy sportsmen gathered for its private trout stream and hunting. Ulysses S. Grant, General William Tecumseh Sherman, and famous restaurateur and caterer Lorenzo Delmonico all frequented the area. The park was eventually opened to the public in 1978.

Start your hike by walking past the parking lot and a pond full of nesting ducks and geese on your right. Keep walking past the Main House, which was used as Snedecor's Tavern in the 1800s, and continue on to the Oakdale Grist Mill. The mill was built in the mid-1700s by the local Nicoll family, founders of the nearby town of Islip.

Continue over the cement bridge that frames the rushing waters of the Connetquot River and hike into the woods. Follow the red arrows, bearing left, and enjoy a wide dirt path with a thick forest on each side. This area of Long Island was called the Pine Barrens by early settlers because trees were lacking and the soil was infertile. Today it's rich with pitch pines, scarlet oaks, white oak, huckleberry, wintergreen, sweet fern, and bracken fern.

Shortly after crossing over a creek, look for a spur trail at 0.2 mile on your left, with access to the pond. Here you should see resident trout and a community of ducks sunbathing near the banks. Continue following the red blazes, make a tight left at 0.7 mile, and hike past the angler fishing area on your left with red arrows pointing straight ahead. At 1.5 miles keep straight and continue over three wooden bridges. Look left to make your way down to the hatchery for a lesson in trout harvesting and watch as its jumping

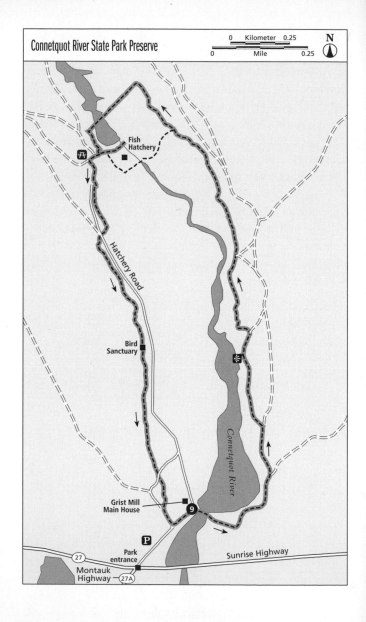

Connetquot River State Park Preserve

0   Kilometer   0.25

0   Mile   0.25

N

Fish Hatchery

Hatchery Road

Bird Sanctuary

Grist Mill Main House

9

P

Park entrance

Montauk Highway

27

27A

Sunrise Highway

Connetquot River

residents peek out of the water looking for a bite of brown spinner or ash-winged large caddis fly.

After your hatchery lesson, walk back over the small wooden bridges leading to the hatchery and look for the yellow blazes. From here, you'll wade out of the woods and cross over Hatchery Road. Keep following along the paved road of the park and take notice of the bird sanctuaries nestled on your right and listen for ring-necked pheasant, ruffed grouse, wild turkey, and northern bobwhite in the area.

Keep following the yellow arrows and cross over another road just before winding around the Main House and park buildings to return to the trailhead.

Miles and Directions

0.0 Start at the Oakdale Grist Mill and walk into the woods to pick up the red trail.

0.2 Look for the spur trail on the left for access to the pond.

0.6 Turn left and walk onto the wooden dock over the pond.

0.7 Make a tight left to stay on the red trail.

1.5 Continue straight at the fork for the red trail.

1.7 Turn left for the trout hatchery.

1.8 Return to the original path from the hatchery and pick up the yellow trail.

2.4 Pass the bird sanctuary on your right.

3.0 End the hike back at the Grist Mill.

10 Stump Pond

Take a walk along the headwaters of the Nissequogue River and explore the shore of a forested pond, an old mill, and tranquil boardwalk crossings.

Distance: 5.4-mile loop
Approximate hike time: 3 hours
Difficulty: Moderate due to length
Trail surface: Gravel and dirt
Best season: Feb through Oct
Other trail users: Joggers
Canine compatibility: Leashed
dogs permitted
Schedule: Dawn until dusk, year-round
Maps: USGS quad: Central Islip
Contact: Blydenburgh County Park, Smithtown; (631) 698-2225; www.suffolkcountyny.gov

Finding the trailhead: Take the Long Island Expressway (I-495) east to exit 42 and merge onto Northern State Parkway East. Drive for 16.5 miles. Continue onto Veterans Memorial Highway/Route 454 to the Blydenburgh Park entrance opposite the H. Lee Dennison County Center in Hauppauge. Follow signs into the park to the boat-launch parking area. The trailhead is to the right of the restrooms. GPS: N40 49.50' / W73 13.20'

The Hike

Stump Pond was named in 1798 when a trio of cousins sought to dam the headwaters of the Nissequogue River for a mill. Their efforts flooded the original banks and formed a pond spanning 180 acres. Over the years swollen tree stumps poked out from the former banks and helped coin the name Stump Pond.

Now part of Blydenburgh County Park, the pond–side scenic trails offer a leisurely stroll around a secluded pond that features swans, water views, wooded terrain, and intersecting horse trails. Pick up the trailhead just to the right of the restrooms, keeping Stump Pond on your left. Start hiking, weaving between spur trails lining the banks or sticking to the wider path just a few feet inland. Continue following the blue blazes and hike east along Lower Lake Trail, taking in the tranquil water views.

Continue to pass by the intersecting spur trails, and at 0.5 mile cross a wooden bridge and continue to a peak of flat terrain jutting into the pond. Swans and geese are common in this area and can be seen gliding on the water throughout the hike. Make a tight right and hike back into the woods, continuing to hug the water's edge. When you trot over the third bridge at the northeast side of the pond, veer left and walk downhill.

Horse trails are plentiful on this side of the park, and taking any of the forks splintering out to your right will lead into winding forest trails popular with equestrians. Keep straight or lean left at the upcoming forks and watch for the glimmering edges of Stump Pond drifting back into view.

When you reach 2.7 miles, bear left and left again at the upcoming intersection and make your way past the old Grist Mill and over a wooden bridge and then keep straight at the upcoming fork. This area of the park features a miller's house, farm cottage, outbuildings, and a 1798 milling center founded by the Smith and Blydenburgh families of Smithtown. Today it's a tranquil stop for hikers and canine companions to play near the water's edge.

Continue winding right and make your way deeper into the woods to cross over a boardwalk. Veer left at 4.7 miles and turn right at the following fork just past the homes.

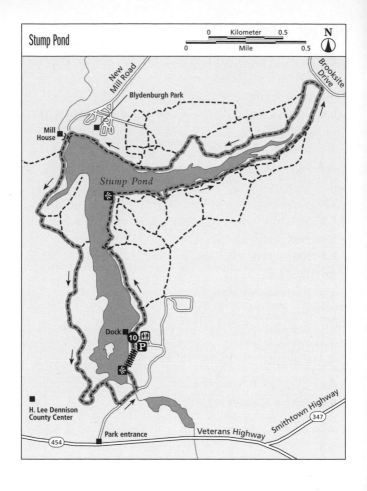

When you hit the park road at 5.0 miles, turn left and follow along the road before picking up the trail again just a few yards ahead. Cross over a final wooden boardwalk and end your hike at the trailhead where you started.

Miles and Directions

0.0 Start at the trailhead adjacent to the restrooms and keep the pond on your left.

0.5 Cross over the wooden bridge.

0.8 Stop for views of the pond and make a sharp right back into the woods.

1.0 Cross over the bridge.

1.9 Cross the wooden bridge.

2.1 Bear left at the fork.

2.7 Bear left and keep left.

3.3 Turn left and pass by Mill House.

3.4 Walk over the bridge.

3.7 Keep straight at the fork.

3.9 Wind right.

4.5 Cross the wooden bridge.

4.7 Turn left.

4.9 Bear right.

5.0 Turn left and follow the park road.

5.1 Turn left.

5.3 Cross over the boardwalk.

5.4 End the hike back at the trailhead.

11 Caleb State Park

Hike through a colonial-inspired Nissequogue River watershed with historic houses, pine barrens, swampy terrain, and views of a sparkling pond on 543 acres of mostly undeveloped terrain.

Distance: 3.0 miles, double loop
Approximate hike time: 2 hours
Difficulty: Easy
Trail surface: Dirt and some paved areas
Best season: Apr through Oct and after a snowfall
Other trail users: Cross-country skiers

Canine compatibility: Dogs not permitted
Schedule: Open year-round from 8:00 a.m. to sunset
Maps: USGS quad: Central Islip
Contact: New York State Office of Parks, Recreation and Historic Preservation, Smithtown; (631) 265-1054; www.nysparks.com/parks

Finding the trailhead: Take the Long Island Expressway (I-495) to exit 53. Follow Sagtikos Parkway for 3.3 miles north to Sunken Meadow Parkway. Continue north for 1.7 miles and take exit SM 3 east to Smithtown. Turn onto Jericho Turnpike/Route 25 east for 3.0 miles to the park, and turn left into the parking lot. GPS: N40 51.11' / W73 13.32'

The Hike

Richard Smythe, a founding father of Smithtown, first came to the area of Caleb State Park, reportedly, after England's King Charles II conveyed the lands to him. Grandson Caleb assisted in disrupting the occupation of British troops on Long Island and was subsequently elected to the state assembly.

Eventually the Brooklyn Gun Club bought the land to serve as a hunting and fishing preserve and called it the Wyandanch Club. The state of New York acquired the land in 1964 and it was changed to Caleb Smith State Park to honor the founding family of Smithtown.

Explore the winding trails of the park by walking past the first driveway of the Nature Center. The restored building was crafted by Caleb's father and given to his son in the mid-1700s as a wedding gift. Today it serves as a nature center and museum complete with exhibits, park information, and historical information.

Ascend the second driveway and make your way left, following the yellow circles with black arrows into the woods. Bear right at the start of your hike and continue left to walk past the open fields, and keep hiking until you reach a fork at 0.1 mile. Hang a right and then another right to follow along with the yellow trail blazes. Take a moment to admire the array of red maples and chokeberry hugging the trails.

At 0.3 mile bear right and continue until you walk through the billowing cedars peppered with black birches leading to the fork located at 0.5 mile. Straight ahead you'll notice the white blazes of the Suffolk Greenbelt Trail. Make a left here and then turn right at the upcoming four-way crossing.

Continue hiking through the towering white pines peppering the downward slope and bear left at the bend onto a dirt service road. Wind right, continue straight, and head over a paved park road. At 1.0 mile bear left and left again at the next intersection. Take note of the lowland swamp area with skunk cabbage and ferns dotting the sandy trail lined with oaks. Keep walking along the swampy stream bed on your left and enjoy the relative calm of the forest punctuated with an occasional call of a songbird.

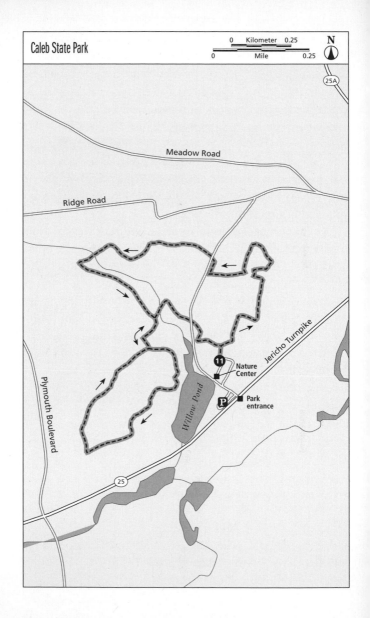

Caleb State Park

0 Kilometer 0.25

0 Mile 0.25

N

25A

Meadow Road

Ridge Road

Jericho Turnpike

Plymouth Boulevard

11 Nature Center

P Park entrance

Willow Pond

25

Walk past the off-limits erosion-control steps and at 1.4 miles bear right to ascend a hill. Jog just a short distance ahead before turning left at the upcoming T-shaped fork. From here, follow along with the corresponding orange blazes. Veer left again and after a brief jaunt watch for Willow Pond to unfold below. On a hot summer day, stop to envy the Canada geese and wood ducks gliding through the cool waters.

Continue following the orange blazes, and wind through the woods until you reach 1.9 miles and hang another right to begin looping back. Keep straight and continue bearing right until your original loop forks at 2.3 miles. From here, hang a left and walk back down the hill you ascended earlier and cross over the wooden bridge.

Cross over two more bridges and look for hints of resident garlic mustard and skunk cabbage surrounding the trail. Continue walking over the paved park road and pick up the yellow discs once again to return to the Nature Center.

Miles and Directions

0.0 Start at the trailhead off the second driveway leading to the Nature Center.

0.1 Bear right at the fork and then make another right.

0.5 Turn left at the fork and right at the upcoming four-way crossing.

1.0 Walk over the paved park road and bear left at the next intersection. Walk past the swamp.

1.4 Walk past the intersection leading to the bridge, bear left, and walk uphill. Look to your left for views of the pond.

1.9 Bear right and loop back to the intersection with the bridge.

2.3 Turn left, then right, and walk over three wooden bridges, making your way back toward the Nature Center.

3.0 End at the trailhead and Nature Center.

12 Sunken Meadow

Discover breathtaking views of the Long Island Sound and explore tidal mud flats, a bird sanctuary, meadows, and woodland slopes.

Distance: 3.0-mile loop
Approximate hike time: 2 hours
Difficulty: Moderate due to a few steep hills
Trail surface: Sand, dirt, and some paved sections
Best season: Mar through Oct
Other trail users: None
Canine compatibility: Dogs permitted on 6-foot leash in undeveloped areas of the park. Dogs are not permitted in bathing or picnic areas, in buildings, park office, or on walkways.
Schedule: Sunrise to sunset, year-round. Closed Mon, except holidays.
Maps: USGS quad: Northport
Contact: Governor Alfred E. Smith/Sunken Meadow State Park, Northport; (631) 269-4333; http://nysparks.state.ny.us

Finding the trailhead: From the Long Island Expressway (I-495), take exit 53 toward Sagtikos Parkway North/Sunken Meadow State Parkway. Continue following signs to Sunken Meadow State Park for approximately 7.3 miles, still heading north. The road ends at the park entrance ticket booth. From here, follow signs to Field #3 and pull up near the beach access point from the lot. GPS: N40 54.34' / W73 14.46'

The Hike

Sunken Meadow was named for a low meadowland separating the beach from an upland forest and was cobbled together from a variety of parcels over the years. Most of its original 520 acres was acquired from Long Island residents George B. Lamb and Antoinette Storrs Lamb. The park has

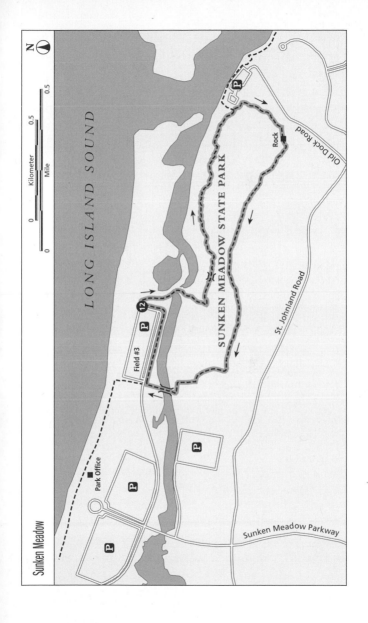

Sunken Meadow

N

LONG ISLAND SOUND

SUNKEN MEADOW STATE PARK

Field #3

Park Office

Rock

Old Dock Road

St. Johnland Road

Sunken Meadow Parkway

Kilometer
0   0.5
0   0.5
Mile

expanded to a staggering 1,200-plus acres over the years and includes a boardwalk, plentiful recreational areas, picnic tables, a golf course, and refreshment kiosks.

For hikers and wildlife enthusiasts, the crowning jewel of the park are its high trails with expansive views of the Long Island Sound. But it doesn't come without a little effort. Start your hike at the beach entrance just off the parking lot. Turn right and make your way around the marshy ponds. Keep bearing left and at 0.2 mile look right for a spur trail leading up a hill into the woods. Although it's a steep climb that will prove difficult in muddy conditions, the journey is well worth the effort. Once you resurface, lean left and watch as sparkling views of the Long Island Sound unfold below.

Ignore the tangle of spur trails and hug the rim trail to enjoy water views. If you're a fan of Long Island parks and preserves, you'll recognize the double white blazes of the Suffolk Greenbelt Trail connecting Sunken Meadow to the Atlantic Ocean in some 30 miles to the south. Other trails remain unmarked and splinter outward from the main trail.

Keep hiking along with the yellow blazes and watch your footing on exposed roots and knobs fingering over the trails. On your left, oaks and chokeberry brush up against its borders. At 0.6 mile a staircase on your left leads to an overlook area of the Long Island Sound. Turn right and ascend a short hill through a snarl of briars, and head inland through the woods.

Bear right at 1.0 mile near St. Johnland Road and pass by a scattering of glacial erratics on your left at 1.2 miles. Continue past the spur forks and trails leading back toward the water's edge until you reach a wide fork at 1.9 miles. Turn right and cut back toward the direction of the water.

When you reach 2.1 miles, walk across the picnic area through the corridor of trees and take a right at 2.3 miles. Walk down a hill and to the arched wooden bridge. This is a prime spot for bird-watching as loons, Canada geese, and snowy egrets congregate around the water's edge. Just over the bridge, you can cut through the woods via a spur trail on your right and explore more of the park's brush and vegetation. Look for wild blackberries and cottontail rabbits resting along the water's edge. Wind back out of the wood and return to the parking lot on your left.

Miles and Directions

0.0 Start near the beach at the Field #3 parking lot and bear right to walk around the marshy pond.

0.2 Look right for the spur trail leading up the hill. Bear left and continue to hike along the rim.

0.6 Turn right and head inland. (**Option:** Turn left to walk down the stairs to the water.)

1.0 Bear right.

1.2 Look at the glacial erratics on your left.

1.9 Turn right at the wide fork.

2.1 Cut through the corridor of trees and the picnic area.

2.3 Turn right and walk down over the bridge.

2.6 Stop at the bridge to look at birds. Turn right after the bridge and head back to the parking lot.

3.0 End the hike back at the Field #3 parking lot.

13 David Weld Sanctuary

Hike through grassy meadows and make your way around a swamp forest. Stop at the shoreline to explore glaciated remains and delve into the woods to leave suburbia behind.

Distance: 3.0-mile loop
Approximate hike time: 2 hours
Difficulty: Easy
Trail surface: Grass, dirt, and sand
Best season: Apr through Oct
Other trail users: None

Canine compatibility: Dogs not permitted
Schedule: Dawn until dusk, year-round
Maps: USGS quad: Central Islip
Contact: Village of Nissequogue, Smithtown; www.nature.org

Finding the trailhead: Take the Long Island Expressway (I-495) to exit 56. Follow Route 111 north and continue for 4.0 miles to Route 25. Cross Route 25, then bear left onto River Road and continue for 3.5 miles, then turn left onto Moriches Road. Continue 0.1 mile onto Horse Race Lane, and after 0.4 mile turn left onto Short Beach Road. Drive 0.1 mile to the entrance on your right. If you hit Smithtown Short Beach, you've gone too far. GPS: N40 54.19' / W73 12.31'

The Hike

David Weld Sanctuary was originally owned by Richard "Bull" Smythe, a name you might recognize from the history surrounding Caleb State Park. Smythe made a deal with a Native American chief in the 1600s so he could ride his pet bull on the property. Eventually the Weld family took over the land and passed most of it on to the Nature Conservancy.

Slip past the iron gate at the parking area and head along the dirt path to the map and information kiosk. Don't forget to grab a map, as you'll pass by a series of discovery stations numbered on hiking posts that correspond to the map.

Continue past the tall, grassy fields and bear left in about 400 feet. The deciduous forests of the sanctuary were born from glacial deposits overlain by a layer of windblown silt called loess. As you wind around the fields into the forest and beyond, look for mulberry tickling the borders of the trail.

Continue hiking and at 0.4 mile, bear left at the fork. Wind your way past residential homes and pay attention to the potent smell permeating from a woodland swamp that houses dense reeds, tall grasses, and skunk cabbage. Pass by a tulip tree with a long trunk and fissured bark, one of the most primitive flowering plants on earth.

At 0.7 mile you can turn left and walk out of the thick canopy forest for beachside views. Locate the small spur trail on your left and climb down. From here, explore the shoreline and the glacial erratics sitting snug to the water's edge. These are rare finds on Long Island and worth a quick hop down the shore. You can make a loop down the beach and then later hang a left to make your way back up onto the main trail and backtrack to the parking lot. But to venture deeper into the woods, reenter the woods you came from and turn left.

Continue walking and turn right at 1.1 miles, delving into the woods to explore more silver-barked beech and towering oaks. Slip through the forest and leave the sounds of the water behind as you edge your way around the private homes that seem to rest smack in the center of the preserve. Turn right at 1.4 miles and walk uphill into

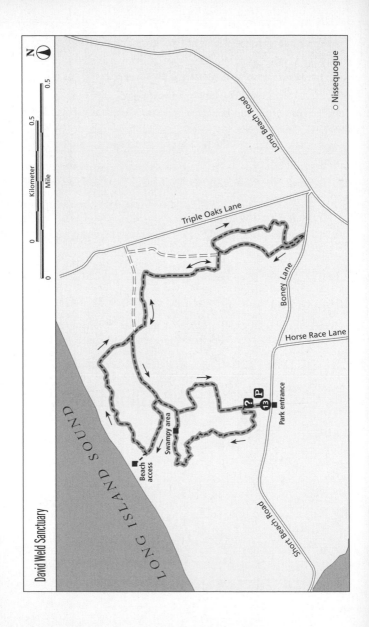

the woods. At 1.7 miles make a left for a short loop back to the main trail. If you continue straight instead, you'll end up at a roadside entrance to the preserve and cut through a residential area.

Finish your short loop and fork to your left at 2.2 miles and then turn left again 0.3 mile later, backtracking the way you came. At 2.7 miles turn left and connect back to the main trail you traversed earlier by bending left at the fork at 3.0 miles. Loop back to the front gate, where you started.

Miles and Direction

0.0 Begin at the gate in the parking area.

0.4 Bear left at the fork.

0.7 Turn left and walk out of the forest for a view of the water. Look for a spur trail on your left if you choose to go down to the shore. Otherwise, backtrack and turn left into the forest.

1.1 Turn right.

1.4 Turn right and walk uphill.

1.7 Turn left and make a short loop back to the main trail.

2.2 Turn left and connect back to the main trail.

2.5 Turn left again and backtrack on your original trail.

2.7 Turn left at the fork.

3.0 End back at the parking area.

14 Prosser Pines Preserve

Saunter through a cathedral forest of white pines and explore one of the country's oldest pine plantations.

Distance: 0.8-mile loop
Approximate hike time: 1 hour
Difficulty: Easy
Trail surface: Gravel and dirt
Best season: Apr through Nov
Other trail users: Joggers
Canine compatibility: Leashed dogs permitted

Schedule: Dawn until dusk, year-round
Maps: USGS quad: Middle Island
Contact: Suffolk County Department of Parks, Middle Island; (631) 854-4949; http://suffolk countyny.gov

Finding the trailhead: Take the Long Island Expressway (I-495) to exit 67 north and continue on Route 21/Yaphank Middle Island Road for 2.9 miles, passing the entrance to Cathedral Pines County Park on your left. Drive for 0.5 mile and turn right into Prosser Pines Preserve. The trailhead is directly adjacent to the parking lot. GPS: N40 52.18' / W72 56.6'

The Hike

One of the oldest surviving pine plantations in the eastern United States, Prosser Pines County Nature Preserve features a cathedral of billowing white pines with a sweet aroma that entices hikers inward to its wide trails.

Prosser Pines' trees were planted in 1812 on Long Island farmland, but their descendants originally hailed from Quebec when war officer Jonathan Edwards brought over seedlings in the mid–1700s. Hurricanes have destroyed much of the original offspring, but mature pines have since sprung up to replace them.

After changing hands to the Daytons in the early 1800s, the land was eventually bought by the Prosser family in 1900. The cathedral of trees was already grown to some 90 feet high, and the new owners were resistant to using it for lumber. The Prosser family would not allow trees to be cut down and hoped the land would one day be preserved as a park. Suffolk County eventually acquired the park in 1968 and honored the Prossers' wishes. Its fifty acres feature a small series of trails and a wide forest path that leads hikers through a glowing green forest of sweet-smelling pine.

Pick up the trailhead directly in front of the parking area and veer right. After a fresh rain, watch as the trees glow in hues of green from dewy pine needles and a blanket of moss. Keep right at the first major fork and stick to the wide forest road to stroll through the corridor of pines.

Follow along parallel to the road before veering left at 0.3 mile to stroll past the neighboring church. Turn left and continue a loop along the wide forest path. You can choose to veer off this lazy loop and turn right up to the open fields, or just take your time strolling through the pine cover.

On a breezy day you might overhear a woodpecker drilling into the trees above. But upon closer inspection, it's just the creek of a tall pine in an otherwise quiet forest. As you make your way around the loop and back toward the trailhead, look for neighboring black birch and a scatter of pink lady slippers, Maryland golden aster, and orange butterfly weed.

Follow the main trail back to the trailhead. If you can't get enough of the tall white pines of Prosser Park, drive over

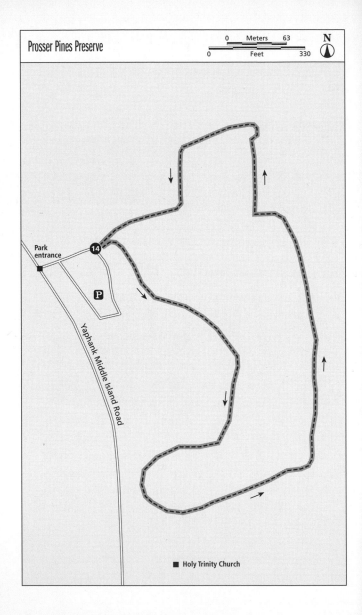

Prosser Pines Preserve

0   Meters   63
0   Feet   330

N

Park
entrance

14

P

Yaphank Middle Island Road

■ Holy Trinity Church

to nearby Cathedral Pines County Park, which you passed on your way in. Its 320 acres feature winding mountain-bike and hiking trails sandwiched between tall pines, a pond, and a streambed.

Miles and Direction

0.0 Start at the trailhead adjacent to the parking lot and bear right at the first major fork.

0.3 Turn left and pass the fenced church.

0.4 Turn left onto the wide path.

0.5 Bear left at the fork.

0.6 Turn right and continue bearing left along the wide forest path.

0.8 End the hike back at the parking lot.

15 Robert Cushman Murphy County State Park

Hike through a watershed for the Peconic River and explore rare coastal plains and pond–shore habitats.

Distance: 3.7-mile loop
Approximate hike time: 2½ hours
Difficulty: Easy
Trail surface: Gravel, dirt, and grass
Best season: Mar through Oct
Other trail users: Fishermen, hunters, and scientists

Canine compatibility: Leashed dogs permitted
Schedule: Dawn until dusk, year-round
Maps: USGS quad: Wading River
Contact: Suffolk County Parks, Manorville; (631) 854-4949; www.suffolkcountyny.gov

Finding the trailhead: Take the Long Island Expressway (I-495) to Wading River Road at exit 69. Continue north on Wading River Road for approximately 1.3 miles to a gravel parking area on the left, adjacent to a trailhead with the white blazes of Paumanok Path. GPS: N40 52.57' / W72 49.36'

The Hike

Named for famed scientist Robert Cushman Murphy, this secluded trail system is Suffolk County's first natural park. Murphy was a respected ornithologist and the American Museum of Natural History's former Lamont curator of birds. His namesake park provides plentiful bird–watching opportunities while licensed fishermen flock to Swan Pond for the impressive array of largemouth bass, yellow perch, bullhead catfish, pumpkinseed sunfish, and eastern chain pickerel.

But fishermen, hikers, and canine companions aren't the only park visitors you'll see on your outdoor journey here. Scientists also come to the area for biological research along the park's rare coastal plains and pond-shore habitats. The nearby Peconic River, the longest on Long Island, provides a watershed for the park and attracts wetland plants and wildlife on its 2,200 acres.

Start your nature hike at the well-marked trailhead adjoining the parking area. Follow the white blazes through a cover of forest litter and wild blueberry grazing against your feet. Take note of the spur trails leading down to Jones Pond just on your left. The hike is straight and narrow before spilling out at a grassy meadow. Bear left and then right at the upcoming sandy woods fork. Cross over the fork and take your second left at 0.7 mile and keep straight through the approaching spur trails down a wooded corridor and encroaching views of Sandy Pond just ahead. Turn right at 1.1 miles and hug the main trail until you see views of Duck Pond. The trail cuts down to Peasys Pond, where you may discover an ankle-deep stream cutting directly across the trail. Look to your right and cross over a makeshift bridge of sturdy sticks and logs. During dry months, just skip over the damp riverbed by foot and watch for nesting bullfrogs.

Hike past a scattering of maple trees and turn left at an upcoming intersection. When you see the white blazes of the Paumanok Path at 2.2 miles, turn left. From here, keep hiking east and skip over a stream connecting Sandy and Grassy Ponds before arriving at a broad T intersection. Turn left and spill onto the banks of Sandy Pond. Bring along a plant or resource guide to study the species edging around the wetland pond.

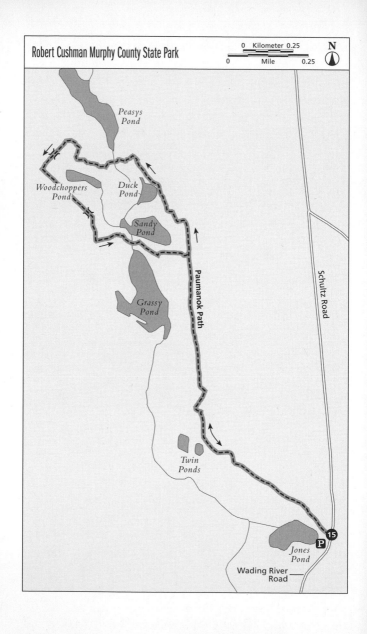

Robert Cushman Murphy County State Park

0 Kilometer 0.25

0 Mile 0.25

N

Peasys Pond

Woodchoppers Pond

Duck Pond

Sandy Pond

Grassy Pond

Paumanok Path

Twin Ponds

Jones Pond

Schultz Road

Wading River Road

P 15

Hike south and follow the white blazes, with views of Grassy Pond over on your right, and pass by Twin and Jones Ponds. Wind back to the original trailhead and enjoy another brush with wild blueberry and mountain laurels.

Miles and Directions

0.0   Start at the trailhead adjacent to the parking area and pass Jones Pond on your left.

0.6   Bear left at the grassy meadow and then right at the upcoming fork.

0.7   Cross over the fork and turn left at the following intersection.

1.1   Turn right and walk past the Duck Pond.

1.2   Turn left at the fork.

1.6   Bear right for the footbridge over a stream.

2.0   Turn left at the three-way intersection and walk down the hilly path.

2.2   Turn left and look for white blazes. Pass by a swamp on your left.

2.3   Walk over the wooden bridge.

2.4   Walk through the clearing and bear left past the lake.

2.5   Turn right and follow blazes through the following intersection. Turn right at the field.

3.7   End the hike back at the parking lot.

16 Long Pond Greenbelt Trail

Hike past the largest pond in the Long Pond Greenbelt and venture through wetlands, ponds, and hardwood forests.

Distance: 3.7-mile loop
Approximate hike time: 2½ hours
Difficulty: Easy
Trail surface: Gravel, dirt, and grass
Best season: Mar through Oct
Other trail users: Joggers

Canine compatibility: Leashed dogs permitted
Schedule: Dawn until dusk, year-round
Maps: USGS quad: Sag Harbor
Contact: Suffolk County Department of Parks, South Hampton; (631) 854-4949; www.suffolk countyny.gov

Finding the trailhead: Take the Long Island Expressway (I-495) east and take exit 68 for William Floyd Parkway. Drive south toward Shirley for 3.5 miles to NY 27 east. Travel east on NY 27 for 55 miles. Turn left at Sagg Road. Drive north for 2.76 miles and turn left onto Round Pond Lane. Park at the end of the cul-de-sac and look for the adjoining trailhead. GPS: N40 59.3' / W72 17.29'

The Hike

The Long Pond Greenbelt features 1,100 acres of wetlands, ponds, and woods from the Peconic Bay to the Atlantic Ocean. Primarily known for its vulnerable ecosystems, the area features coastal plain ponds and more than thirty rare species of plants and animals. Its nearly one hundred different bird species rely on the wetland communities nestled in this corridor.

The region was carved by a glacial advance and retreat that created moraines stretching across the entire length of

Long Island. Named for the largest pond in the Long Pond Greenbelt, the trail resides just south of the village of Sag Harbor. Hikers can cruise past its interconnecting ponds and forest while crossing a forgotten railway that once connected Bridgehampton to Sag Harbor.

Start at the trailhead directly adjacent to the parking area and hike past Round Pond just on your right. A connection between the upcoming railroad spur and the Round Pond Icehouse was once used to ship ice to New York City. Continue past the scatter of homes and bear left at the first fork. Watch for local scarlet, white, and black oak while continuing straight until crossing over Ligonee Brook. From here, continue until you reach an intersection with the Old Sag Harbor Railroad spur.

The railroad ran from 1870 until 1939 and was eventually dismantled and recycled for its steel during World War II. All that's left today is a dirt-strewn railroad bed, ideal for a day of hiking. Hang a left and pass by Little Long Pond to your left. Cross over Sprig Tree Path and under the blanket of suburban power lines.

During your hike, notice the staccato spurts of punctuated hilly terrain, offering a more strenuous workout for an otherwise flat trail. At 0.9 mile look for a wooden rail fence and turn left to a path for Crooked Pond. Hike down to the pond and turn left at your first fork to head northeast on Crooked Pond Trail. From here, enjoy views of the water and surrounding terrain, hardly aware of encroaching civilization. Sit quietly and watch for eastern tiger salamanders scurrying past.

When you reach 1.1 miles, turn left on Sprig Tree Path and look for the glimmer of water from Deer Drink Pond in the distance. From here, you'll pass twice over

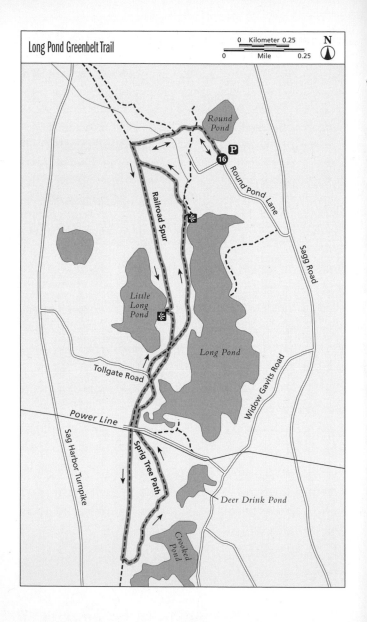

Long Pond Greenbelt Trail

0   Kilometer 0.25
0   Mile   0.25

N

Round Pond

P
16

Round Pond Lane

Sagg Road

Railroad Spur

Little Long Pond

Long Pond

Tollgate Road

Widow Gavits Road

Power Line

Sag Harbor Turnpike

Sprig Tree Path

Deer Drink Pond

Crooked Pond

spur trails and find yourself joined with the white blazes of Paumanok Path before reaching Long Pond. Take a break at the northern tip of Long Pond and admire the stretch of water, looking for rare plant species ranging from knotted spikerush and red-root flatsedge to long-tubercled plants, before continuing north along Sprig Tree Path.

Take a right at the rail bed and then another immediate right to pick up Round Pond Trail. Pass back over Ligonee Brook and return to the trailhead where you started.

Miles and Directions

0.0 Start at the trailhead adjacent to the parking area.

0.1 Bear left at the fork.

0.4 Turn left onto the old railroad spur.

0.9 Turn left just past the wooden fence for Crooked Pond.

1.1 Turn left on Sprig Tree Path.

2.5 Turn right at the rail bed and make another immediate right for Round Pond Trail. Backtrack to the trailhead.

3.7 End the hike back at the trailhead.

17 Mashomack Preserve–Sanctuary Pond Loop

Take a hike through the "Jewel of the Peconic" and explore 2,039 acres of tidal creeks, fields, freshwater marshes, and mature oak woodlands.

Distance: 5.5-mile loop

Approximate hike time: 4 hours

Difficulty: Moderate due to length

Trail surface: Gravel, dirt, and grass

Best season: Apr through Oct

Other trail users: Hikers

Canine compatibility: Dogs not permitted

Schedule: Dawn until dusk, year-round

Maps: USGS quad: Greenport

Contact: The Nature Conservancy, Shelter Island; (631) 749-1001; www.nature.org

Finding the trailhead: From the Long Island Expressway (I-495) east, take exit 73 for Old Country Road toward Greenport for 0.8 mile. Turn left at Old Country Road/Route 58 and drive 2.3 miles. Take the second exit at Roanoke Avenue and stay on Old Country Road/Route 58 for 1.3 miles to Main Road/NY 25. Continue for 20 miles and take a right at NY 114 for 0.1 mile to the ferry. Once on Shelter Island, follow Route 114 south for 3.0 miles to the preserve entrance. You can also reach the island via the South Ferry from Sag Harbor. Drive 1.0 mile, heading north on Route 114, and turn east into the preserve. GPS: N41 3.25', W72 19.24'

The Hike

Start your journey adjacent to the east visitor center after picking up a color-coded map from the kiosk, and head to the trailhead sign just off the wooden boardwalk. For a quick jaunt, stroll down the boardwalk on your right for 0.2 mile to take in a rare pine swamp dotted with swamp azaleas and highbush blueberries.

Bear right and cruise past red maple, dogwood, and black locust trees scattered along the outskirts of the trail. Hang a left up the stairs made of wood and dirt and wind back downhill. Pass by the observation area overlooking Kettle Pond and continue following the red arrows to the Yellow Trail.

Keep following the red arrows and venture past cinnamon fern, northern bayberry, and poison ivy. Keep right at the next fork and make your way uphill. Hike past the observation area at 0.6 mile and enjoy views of the Shelter Island Sound on your right. After walking over a wooden boardwalk with open fields on either side, cross a dirt road at 0.8 mile onto a sandy path that leads through expansive grassy meadows and intersecting ski trails. Parts of this area are overgrown with Japanese bayberry, a destructive tree that was brought to the area for ornamental value in 1875.

Continue to follow the yellow arrows and pick up the Green Trail at 1.0 mile. Cross a dirt road at 1.2 miles and make your way uphill. Stop for a break, enjoying the water views, and take note of the visiting swans circling a small pond downhill on your right. Keep hiking and skip down the wooden steps, stopping at the wooden lookout shelter on your right for some serene bird-watching.

At 1.9 miles bear right onto another dirt road and watch for cars as you make your way past maintenance buildings and park offices. Just as you leave these buildings behind, walk in between a coastal salt pond on your right, followed by Sanctuary Pond on your left and Bass Creek on your right.

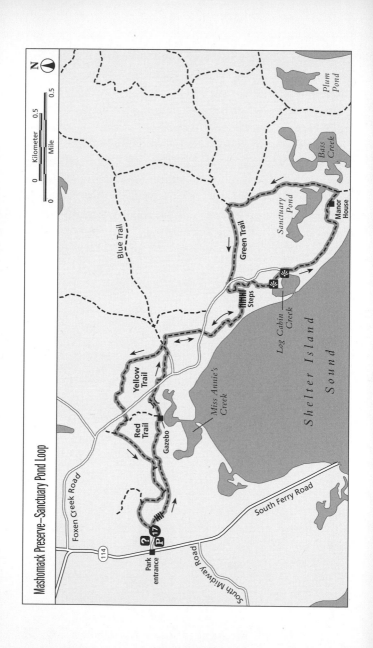

Mashomack Preserve—Sanctuary Pond Loop

Stay on the main path and continue following the green trail markers to begin the second leg of your journey. At 3.4 miles walk up the dirt stairs and bear right on the dirt road followed by a quick jog to the left in about forty paces. Bear right and wind back up the wooden steps while keeping an eye out for a reappearance of those stunning water views.

Cross over two more dirt roads and once you return back into the large open fields, leave the backtracking of the green markers behind and once again pick up the yellow arrows. At 4.6 miles follow the familiar red trail blazes and wind right past the tall birch trees peppering the forest borders. Stroll through the northern edge of the preserve and return to the visitor center where you started.

Miles and Directions

0.0 Start at the trailhead sign east of the visitor center.

0.2 Stay right at the fork.

0.3 Stay right at the fork and wind uphill.

0.6 Pass the observation area and pick up the Yellow Trail.

0.8 Cross the dirt road.

1.0 Bear right and then left to pick up the green-blazed trail.

1.2 Cross over the dirt road.

1.9 Bear right on the dirt road and walk toward the park buildings.

3.4 Walk up the steps and cross the dirt road to your right.

4.1 Bear right to follow the yellow arrows and enter the field.

4.6 Cross over the dirt road and bear right to pick up the Red Trail.

5.5 End the hike back at the visitor center.

18 Cedar Point Lighthouse

This delightful hike will take you through a forest to bluffs overlooking Gardiners Bay before reaching a former shipping port and an aging lighthouse.

Distance: 5.4-mile loop
Approximate hike time: 3 hours
Difficulty: Moderate due to length and some hills
Trail surface: Gravel, dirt, and sand
Best season: May through Oct
Other trail users: Joggers

Canine compatibility: Leashed dogs permitted
Schedule: Dawn until dusk, year-round
Maps: USGS quad: Greenport
Contact: Suffolk County Department of Parks, East Hampton; (631) 854-4949; www.suffolk countyny.gov

Finding the trailhead: Take the Long Island Expressway (I-495) east to exit 68 for William Floyd Parkway. Drive south toward Shirley for 3.7 miles to NY 27 east. Follow NY 27 for about 60 miles, and turn left onto Stephen Hands Path. Continue for 2.0 miles and cross over Route 114. At 3.4 miles, bear left onto Old Northwest Road and drive approximately 2.0 miles. Bear right onto Northwest Road and park adjacent to the entrance and park office. GPS: N41 1.56' / W72 13.37'

The Hike

Settled in 1651, Cedar Point was once a bustling shipping port from where timber, fish, and farm goods were brought from Sag Harbor to East Hampton. The original lighthouse was a 35–foot-tall wooden tower and was thought to be too fragile for a cast–iron lantern. A granite lighthouse was built in 1869 to help guide whaling ships in the harbor. It once stood some 600 feet from shore before a hurricane shifted the shoreline in 1938 and created a small stretch of land reaching out to the bay. Today the nearly forgotten lighthouse has fallen into decay and rests between the Northwest Harbor and Gardiners Bay.

Folklore of the region and of lighthouse keepers abounds. Local legend has it that Charles Mulford, a keeper here in 1897, lost a leg in the Civil War and subsequently bought up all the wooden peg legs in the area. After a vandal fire in 1974, rumors festered that a firefighter found a storage room full of charred wooden legs buried deep within the lighthouse.

Another keeper, William H. Follet, worked here from 1917 until the light was decommissioned in 1934. He tried in vain to save doomed men from a burning ship called the Flyer, but none survived. Rumors suggest that he was involved in rum-running during Prohibition and hung a lantern on a nearby cedar tree if the Coast Guard was patrolling nearby.

While the lighthouse has long since fallen into disarray, the hike back through history is still vibrant. Start at the trailhead just off the parking lot and park office building. Venture onto the dirt trail, following the yellow blazes, and hike north through pitch pines, chestnut oaks, and wild blueberry. Keep straight on the grassy path, and veer left at 0.8 mile to meet the high, sandy bluffs overlooking Gardiners Bay.

After admiring the views, head left and turn right at the intersection with a wide dirt road. Follow it to the edges of Cedar Beach. While there are no longer cedar trees growing in this area, they once framed the ocean landscape. Turn left

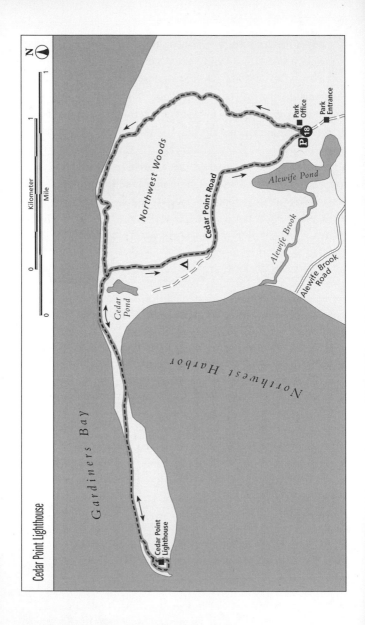

Cedar Point Lighthouse

N

Gardiners Bay

Cedar Point Lighthouse

Cedar Pond

Northwest Harbor

Northwest Woods

Cedar Point Road

Alewife Pond

Alewife Brook

Alewife Brook Road

Park Office

Park Entrance

P 18

0   1
Kilometer

0   1
Mile

for a mile-long journey down to the tip of the beach, where the lighthouse is waiting to greet you.

The boxy, granite structure is tattered from vandalism and has been worn by the weather over the years, but its charm is still evident. Imagine its glory during Mulford's reign as keeper of both the lighthouse and a surplus of wooden legs.

After enjoying the views while circling its landing, backtrack to the beach and hike back to the intersection with the dirt road you traversed earlier. Turn right and hike through the campground until you hit the paved Cedar Point Road at 4.7 miles. Turn left and walk along the edge of the park road, passing by spur trails leading down to the cool waters of Alewife Pond. Continue southeast and back to the parking lot where you started.

Miles and Directions

- **0.0** Start at the trailhead in front of the parking area.
- **0.3** Keep straight at the fork.
- **0.8** Veer left and walk along the rim for views of Gardiners Bay.
- **2.9** Arrive at Cedar Point Lighthouse. Turn around here to retrace your steps back east.
- **4.2** Turn right after the pond and walk down the dirt road through the campground.
- **4.7** Wind right to the paved road and turn left to walk back to the main entrance.
- **5.4** Arrive back at the trailhead.

19 The Walking Dunes

Walk through towering sand dunes that stretch to 80 feet tall, venture through an ominous phantom forest, and learn the mystery of the forever-shifting terrain.

Distance: 0.8-mile loop
Approximate hike time: ½ hour
Difficulty: Easy
Trail surface: Sand and beach
Best season: Mar through Nov
Other trail users: None
Canine compatibility: Leashed dogs permitted

Schedule: Year-round, sunrise to sunset
Maps: USGS quad: Gardiners Island East
Contact: Hither Hills State Park; (631) 668-2554; http://nysparks.state.ny.us

Finding the trailhead: Drive east on Route 27/Sunrise Highway to Montauk Highway and continue about 9.0 miles past Amagansett. From Montauk Highway/Route 27, turn left onto Napeague Harbor Road and drive about 3.0 miles and over the railroad trestle. Drive north approximately 0.75 mile and park at the end of the road. The trailhead is directly adjacent to the information and map kiosk at the end of the road. GPS: N41 0.40' / W72 2.16'

The Hike

This brief hike in Hither Hills State Park may be short on distance, but it's teeming with unexpected terrain and intrigue. The park's active parabolic dune fields are continually shifting southeast and uncovering a forgotten forest. Find out for yourself by turning right onto the trailhead and hiking through mixed oak, bearberry, and pitch pine. And beware of lingering poison ivy.

Just a few feet into the trail, a crushing sand dune greets visitors with a towering stance. The trail bends to the right and makes a gradual ascent up the dunes and onto flat ground. Adventurers should be advised not to run up the dunes, as it furthers erosion and damages the American beach grass that helps stabilize the dunes.

During your hike keep following the trail markers, which are numbered 1 through 10. If you grabbed a map at the information kiosk at the trailhead, you can follow along with the relating information for each marker. Look for red-tailed hawks, osprey, rabbit, deer, and red fox on your journey. Visitors should also look for hitchhiking dog ticks and deer ticks. While vegetation is relatively unvaried along the sand dunes, they are home to beach plum, bayberry, and beach heather. Take a closer look at the color of the sand. If it appears to give off a purple and black hue, it's not the magical mystery of the dunes and abandoned forest. Minerals streaking the sand accounts for its vivid discoloration.

There is an intriguing reason why the area lacks more forest and vegetation. Discover the secret by making your way to trail marker 8. From here, make your way into the Phantom Forest, which was once home to a thriving community of trees and vegetation. Over time its dead trees and trunks were completely buried by sand and gradually uncovered as the dunes shifted southeast. Unknowing or thoughtless visitors came for wood or keepsakes and helped aid in clearing out the stumpy forest.

Stop to take a look at the freshwater wetland bog found at trail marker 9. Seasonally, you might see cranberry plants and wild orchids just a little further ahead. This cranberry bog leads out of the Phantom Forest and down to the beach of Napeague Harbor at marker 10. You can stop here to

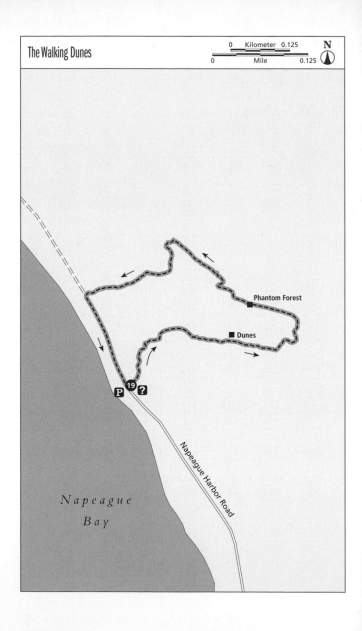

The Walking Dunes

0   Kilometer   0.125

0   Mile   0.125

N

Phantom Forest

■ Dunes

P 19 ?

Napeague Harbor Road

Napeague
Bay

explore the beach and shorebirds at Napeague Bay. Turn left on the beach and make the short hike back to the parking area.

Miles and Directions

0.0 Start at the trailhead adjacent to the parking area.

0.3 Ascend uphill (counterclockwise on the trail) to the top of the dunes and look over the park and harbor.

0.4 Enter the Phantom Forest.

0.7 Turn left and enter the beach.

0.8 End at the trailhead and walk back to your car.

20 Montauk Point State Park

Travel to the tip of Long Island and walk along the beach to watch local seals sunbathing. Try your luck for hidden treasure at Money Pond, and end at a picture-perfect lighthouse on the Atlantic.

Distance: 4.4-mile loop
Approximate hike time: 3 hours
Difficulty: Moderate due to length and some hills
Trail surface: Sand, dirt, and paved
Best season: Apr through Oct
Other trail users: Hikers and beachcombers
Canine compatibility: Dogs permitted on leash no longer than

6 feet. Dogs are not allowed in camping areas, bathing areas, picnic areas, buildings, or on walkways.
Schedule: Open daily year-round from sunrise to sunset.
Maps: USGS quad: Montauk Point OE E
Contact: Montauk Point State Park, Montauk; (631) 668-3781; http://nysparks.state.ny.us

Finding the trailhead: Take the Long Island Expressway (I-495) east to exit 68 for William Floyd Parkway/NY 46, heading toward Shirley, for 0.7 mile. Merge onto NY 46 and take the ramp onto Route 27E after 2.8 miles. Continue driving east for 27.9 miles and turn left at Route 27. After 10.6 miles, turn left at Main Street/Route 27 and continue to Montauk Point State Park. Park near the lighthouse and walk to the trailhead just left of the visitor center and lighthouse. GPS: N41 4.17' / W71 51.30

The Hike

Montauk rests in the region known as Block Island and features a tantalizing past. The notorious pirate Captain William Kidd left hidden treasure on nearby Gardiners

Island, but it was recovered in 1699 after his arrest. Local folklore tells of Kidd hiding two more chests of bounty in the "bottomless" Money Pond. Today fishermen can drop their hooks and hope for a fresh catch . . . or perhaps a bit of gold.

The diversity of Montauk Point is inspiring and unlike any other hike in the region. It ranges from flat beach terrain to woodland hills and inspired water views. To get the best overview of what Montauk Point State Park offers, start your hike at the front of the lighthouse and visitor center. Access the trailhead to the beach just to the left of the visitor center and slope down to the rocky shoreline below. Even on a chilly day, the beach can be appreciated for its dazzling array of colored rocks, rainbow of pebbles, crumbling seashells, and patches of purple-hued sand. Continue hiking parallel to the water and past the spur trails leading inland.

When you reach 0.6 mile, look for the sign indicating the access trail to the seal observation area on your left. You'll need to make a brief, but steep, climb up and walk inland. Wear some comfortable shoes with adequate traction as the paths can get muddy and cover well-worn roots. Keep following the trail markers and bear right. Notice how quickly the park graduated from an expansive seashore to wooded terrain.

At 1.0 mile hike straight past the fork and make your way to unobstructed views of Montauk's esteemed seaside residents. Hooded, ringed, harp, gray, and harbor seals can be found resting on the rocks just beyond the shoreline and draw crowds year-round.

Backtrack to the trail you started from and make a right at 1.7 miles to hike out to Oyster Pond and maneuver through the tall weeds and marshy terrain, making your

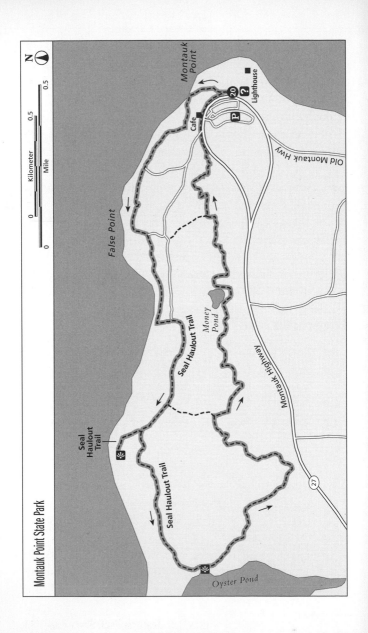

Montauk Point State Park

N

Kilometer
0   0.5
0   0.5
Mile

Montauk Point

Lighthouse

Cafe

P

?
20

False Point

Old Montauk Hwy

Seal Haulout Trail

Money Pond

Seal Haulout Trail

Montauk Highway

Seal Haulout Trail

Oyster Pond

27

way inland. At 2.2 miles look right for a view of the pond. Continue hiking until you reach 3.1 miles, where you'll turn right at the fork. From here, walk down part of the Seal Haulout Trail to pick up Money Pond Trail, which is marked with green blazes.

After climbing over intermittent hills and dealing with some narrow footing, hikers are rewarded with a breathtaking view of the shoreline and forest at 3.5 miles. You might even spot a white-tailed deer, red-tailed hawk, northern black racer snake, or great egret.

Look for the shore and lighthouse peeking through the trees at around 4.2 miles, and walk to the paved road and turn left. From here, turn left and walk past the cafe, or pop inside for a cold drink and enjoy it on their outdoor back deck with views of the beach.

Miles and Directions

0.0 Locate the trailhead to the left of the lighthouse.

0.6 Step up the steep incline to your left to access the Seal Haulout trail and observation area.

1.0 Turn right for the Seal Haulout Trail.

1.7 Return to the main trail and make a right for Oyster Pond Trail.

2.2 Hike past Oyster Pond.

3.1 Bear right and walk down the Seal Haulout Trail to the Money Pond Trail.

3.2 Bear left for the Money Pond Trail.

3.5 Look for Money Pond on your left.

4.2 Watch for the lighthouse to come into view and turn left onto the paved path.

4.4 End the hike back at the lighthouse.

About the Author

Susan Finch is a freelance writer and hiker who specializes in budget, family, and recreational travel. She is the author of *Best Easy Day Hikes Columbus,* and her work has appeared in regional and national outlets. When she's not writing and traveling from her home in Brooklyn, New York, she and her husband, Drew, are planning their next big hiking trip.

WHAT'S SO SPECIAL ABOUT UNSPOILED, NATURAL PLACES?

Beauty   Solitude   Wildness   Freedom   Quiet   Adventure
Serenity   Inspiration   Wonder   Excitement
Relaxation   Challenge

There's a lot to love about our treasured public lands, and the reasons are different for each of us. Whatever your reasons are, the national **Leave No Trace** education program will help you discover special outdoor places, enjoy them, and preserve them—today and for those who follow. By practicing and passing along these simple principles, you can help protect the special places you love from being loved to death.

THE PRINCIPLES OF **LEAVE NO TRACE**

- 🐾 Plan ahead and prepare
- 🐾 Travel and camp on durable surfaces
- 🐾 Dispose of waste properly
- 🐾 Leave what you find
- 🐾 Minimize campfire impacts
- 🐾 Respect wildlife
- 🐾 Be considerate of other visitors